What Not To Date

Alexandra Khan

Fulton Books, Inc.
Meadville, PA

Published by Fulton Books 2020

Edited by Denise Callejas

ISBN 978-1-64952-042-5 (paperback)
ISBN 978-1-64952-043-2 (digital)

Printed in the United States of America

In memory of my dear friend Anastasia

Dear Goldie!

Thank you very much
for your kindness &
card. So happy to
have met you & to me
Enjoy your life to my
fullest. Life is beautiful.

Faty

Contents

Acknowledgments

A VERY SPECIAL THANKS TO my parents and two brothers for everything they have done for me—for the love, affection, care and for teaching me about a lot, inspiring me, and supporting me with my every decision. I am grateful immensely to my parents.

Dreams are impossible to realize without the support of your family and loyal friends. Friends are your chosen family. Fortunately, I surround myself with real people, amazing friends, and talented colleagues. Throughout my journey, I met a lot of good people and made friends. My dear friends with a good core and beautiful hearts are always there for me at my worst, even when I hit rock bottom. Hitting rock bottom was the best thing that ever happened to me. You really get to know who your loyal friends are.

Special acknowledgment to Julia and Galina for their generous soul and kindness; Lola and Emmanuel for welcoming me to Miami; Laura for being there always for me; Javier for his wisdom and mentorship; Ramon for believing in me and instilling trust in me; Manuel, Marvin, and Alejandro for their support and for being great friends; Tatyana and Vladislav for their ingenuity; Olga and Manuel for being the coolest; and Jenny for being a very understanding and fun person. The deepest gratitude to my editor, Denise, for her incredible talent and for being a brilliant, highly intelligent, and kind person.

I hope you can relate to my stories and laugh, learn, and enjoy the happiness of pursuit. Everything great happens with the right person at the right time.

Be happy and healthy!

Introduction

I CAME TO THE USA sixteen years ago. The diversity of cultures and abundance of genetically modified organisms-injected products, cheeses, sausages, tropical fruits, seafood, and humongous portions excited and shocked me. Back home, you got only two types of cheese and sausage but plenty of organic veggies and fruits and natural beef and poultry. In my family, we always had plenty of homemade Korean and Russian food at home. My parents would not go out for dinner for two reasons: my dad loved my mom's cooking, and eating out was not in our culture. Our culture is to host dinners at home; my parents would host dinners once a month and get invited to dinner by our relatives and my parents' best friends. Wives and moms adorably competed for the title of best cook and hostess. As a country, Uzbekistan stands out as the most hospitable and friendliest country of all other former USSR nations. Great hospitality is in our blood. Everyone's a VIP in our home.

The former USSR was a multicultural and diverse country: Greeks, Koreans, Uzbeks, Russians, Azerbaijanis, Russian Jews, Germans, Armenians, and more. Among them were humble, literate, and enthusiastic people who got along very well. Every time my mom cooked a traditional Korean dish, she shared it with our neighbors. They would do the same. As we were a multicultural country, we opened our palates to all the cuisines and dishes: Uzbek, Russian, Greek, Turkish, and Armenian.

Three years after the USSR collapsed, non-Uzbeks were migrating to Canada, Israel, Greece, and Germany. Major corporations, foreign investors, and companies rushed to expand their markets all over the vast country. This period of transition known as *perestroika* proved interesting for all generations. For the older generation, perestroika was a time of uncertainty and confusion. For millennials, it was the greatest opportunity to learn about entrepreneurship, discover inner talents, and become successful. For all of us, the process of adjustment was challenging and exciting at the same time.

The opportunities were limitless for college graduates such as me. Working for the European Union project on strengthening labor policies and statistics was an eye-opening experience that enriched my life. I remember being intellectually stimulated while translating precisely and impressively in front of doctors, biogenetic engineers, and local vineyard owners.

As my two-year contract with the European Union project came to an end, I kept an eye on other EU projects. I had the most profound experience with the EU; I learned a lot and met very highly intellectual people. By pure accident, I met the general manager of Sheraton Uzbekistan at a supermarket where he needed help with English-Russian translations. He asked me to send him my résumé. A few days later, I got a job as a sales manager. The general manager and director of sales and marketing welcomed me with wide open arms, trained me for sales, and instilled trust in me. Thanks to his inspiration and mentorship, I knew I had found my passion. The moment I stepped into the hotel lobby—full of people, laughter, happy guests and employees—I finally understood the saying that being in the right place at the right time and meeting the right person is your chance. I love what I do and consider myself a fundamentally happy person. All I am missing is to find the right person for me, and I can't wait to fall in love.

Hospitality connects people of all cultures all over the world in a very sincere way. Getting to know one's culture, sharing food, and genuine hospitality bring us together. Sharing your stories with your families and friends over homemade dinner and tea with dessert is still the most favorite tradition of all. We often visited our friends and relatives only if they were great hosts and cooks. When you hear "Come over and be my guest," it means you are very welcomed at our house anytime and we like you. Similarly, the more hospitable you are, the better chance you have when it comes to finding a good date. The way you treat guests shows how generous or stingy, mean or nice, and caring or careless you are. Dating is easier with men who appreciate and love at the same level of hospitality as you. For instance, the way you pour tea to your guests and your man reflects the level of attentiveness you are willing to give. And as we all know, men love to get affection and attention from women.

The approval of my parents is important and respected always. There are three things my parents always consider and look at when I introduce a boyfriend: genetics, reputation, and hospitality. Genetics is vital for Koreans. We still trace our bloodlines. I recall my grandfather telling me about our family tree. My great-great-grandfather was Lee San, the son of the twenty-second ruler from the Joseon dynasty (fourteenth to nineteenth century)—a fact that I am proud of immensely. So when it comes to introducing your boyfriend to your family, the first question parents ask is about his family, mother's reputation, genetics, and education credentials. I believe that genetics, culture, and family upbringing play a crucial role in shaping one's individuality, strong intellect, and the relentless pursuit of one's dreams. All these factors represent an immense value. My upbringing was very conservative and strict, but my childhood and adolescence were full of love, meaningful experiences, and warm relationships with my parents.

We lived in a small village where you sneezed on one side of the street and neighbors heard you at the other end. Rumors traveled at the speed of light. Living in a small village has its advantages and disadvantages. It creates a sense of community. It's easy to find a babysitter. You have your neighbors and cousins and grandparents to help with that. Everyone knows everything about you, and everyone knows your business. The disadvantage comes for those few characters and individuals whose reputation gets stained.

One such interesting character in our village was a very influential politician, a married man in his midforties with four children who was also going out with four women at the same time. Apparently, he had one mistress for sex, one mistress to show off because she was strikingly beautiful (although she used him to meet very highly influential and powerful men), another mistress for intellectual stimulation, and a fourth mistress who was married but very wealthy. All four women and wife gathered and entrapped him in a hotel room for days with very little food and isolated him from the entire world. A few days later, his wife divorced him and all his mistresses disappeared. He was left with nothing.

I remember my mom saying, "Reputation is everything. You must protect and maintain a stellar reputation from an early age. Be a good and decent person—earn respect." When it comes to girls, Koreans look at a girl's mother. I did not understand then, for example, why my mom never let me sleepover at my friend's place; it was because her mom had been cheating on her husband and sleeping around.

My dad was a gastroenterology surgeon and second in charge at a regional hospital in Uzbekistan. In the early '90s, hospitals received humanitarian aid from the American Red Cross. It turned out, the chief of the regional hospital was selling medical supplies to the patients illegally. He had sold enough to build a house. My dad demanded he stop selling and get to work. His boss's ego was hurt, and he took revenge by badmouthing my dad. The moment my mom heard about it, her petite five-foot frame rushed to his house, grabbed him by his neck, and said, "If you talk bad about my husband and stain his reputation, I will shoot your dishonest ass and your children." The tall and overweight hospital chief was stuttering, and he almost shit in his pants. My mom always protected the entire family and stood by my dad. Patience, compassion, respect, trust, and love for each other and their children were what made our family the happiest and strongest.

People were humble and trustworthy back then; we used to leave our house keys to our neighbors when we traveled for vacation. If any of our friends or relatives needed any help, friends, family, and colleagues helped instantly. I remember seeing dozens of boxes of honeydews, watermelons, and apples and rice left at the front door of our house, most often gestures of gratitude on behalf of my dad's patients.

I am immensely proud of my dad who would stand up on his feet for six to eight hours saving lives and performing surgeries. It was his calling and his passion to cure and make people healthy. Given the poor conditions of Soviet Union-era hospitals, my father always was ready to help his patients no matter what time he got called in. Back then, doctors made pennies compared to American standards, but my dad was always so happy to rush to the hospital. All he had was a medical education, passion for his profession, and desire to cure his patients. In the hearts of many people, my father had the most beautiful heart, mind, and golden hands. That was why my mom fell in love with my dad.

My mom was the most giving person I have ever known. She was always giving away food and clothes to our neighbors and families with a lot of kids. In late '80s Uzbekistan, there were families with five or more children. My mom was always cooking and taking care of us. What made my mom happy was

13

the joy of making her delicious meals, throwing the best kids' birthday parties, health, dancing, and togetherness. Her purpose in life was my dad, my older brothers, and me. My mom did everything possible to make everyone happy. Even though my mom had a rough childhood—raised her little sister on her own and was left by her elder brother and took care of my cousins—she remained the kindest, most giving, generous, and best mom in the world. That was why my dad fell in love with my mom deeply.

My parents taught me how to maintain and earn a good reputation from an early stage of life—be compassionate, supportive, and take care of each other under any circumstances. My mom and dad got married with four oranges, a bottle of champagne, and wedding rings made of wire. They went through ups and downs and rough times and stuck together till the last days of their lives. We celebrated the fiftieth anniversary of my parents' marriage in 2009. It was the most beautiful, emotional, and joyful family gathering.

As an adult, I cherish these memories for the rest of my life. All precious memories put a big smile on my face even when I have a dreadful day. I am very thankful to my parents for everything they have taught me.

The first city I moved to from Uzbekistan was New York. As the saying goes, "If you can make it here, you can make it anywhere." That was one of the motivators-activators that moved me straight from conservative Uzbekistan to an entirely different planet—New York City. I wanted to experience this city of contrasts and dynamic rhythm.

What I soon discovered was that people in New York were not hospitable at all. I remember the reaction of my coworkers when I would offer to share my lunch with them. Apparently, that was not a typical gesture in New York. The fact that people did not even share food with their roommates was a cultural shock for me.

I landed a job with one of the top twenty hotels in the world. My responsibilities were to create a flawless experience for high-end guests by providing impeccable service as their primary point of contact. It was a learning experience and a boot camp for three and a half years. Nobility among the rich and famous is rare to find. At a five-star hotel, the wealthy and famous can't wait. They want it now, not a second later. The richer, the more demanding and the more stingy and nasty they get. Only a few wealthy people demonstrated nobility and high class.

Frankly speaking, my first job was very tough and challenging. Starting from scratch and working from the bottom all the way up was thrilling to me. I had to adjust, or I'd lose my valuable time and opportunities. To make it in the US, I had to learn a lot, fuel up with patience and tenacity, and be smart about every move. My plan was to work in hotel operations for a year, gain experience, learn about the hotel market, and get back in hotel sales. Undoubtedly, it is achievable. I am determined to make it big in the hotel industry in the USA and meet someone who would appreciate hospitality and who is hardworking and ambitious and attractive. Someone who loves to travel, cook, and read and loves what he does for a living and overall is an interesting person to be around. There is one for me on this continent.

We all want happiness, and we all want to find that person even if it takes us to cross the entire Atlantic Ocean.

CHAPTER 1

Love at First Sight and Other Drugs

DATING IN NYC IS TOUGH. The competition is fierce. You see gorgeous and impressively dressed men walking with swagger in Midtown Manhattan, Wall Street, and Times Square. I observed how they walk. They keep a straight posture and their chin up. The confident and powerful walk is very attractive and sexy.

There is no place like New York! In my words and from my experience, New York is the center of art. It's the capital of the financial world, entertainment, fashion and food mecca of the USA, and much more.

To my biggest surprise, the guys I dated in New York were know-it-alls and uninteresting. I thought they would be so upbeat, entertaining, and enthusiastic. Logically, I always remembered guys by their occupation. Some people, I noticed, chose their occupations based on the level of temper, the scope of work, the level of laziness and talents. Some of them were bellmen, real estate agents, greedy bankers, and generous lawyers with small wieners. There are good guys out there, but it is hard to meet them.

After my best friend, Julia, left for California, I got a new friend and roommate. Anastasia was Russian; she was a beautiful, highly intelligent, very strong, honest, and opinionated person. Her parents are wonderful people. What I loved about her was she never got jealous over your success or jealous of the great and rich boyfriends of her girlfriends. It is rare to find a sincere and highly intellectual friend. I was very lucky to have met Anastasia.

Every time I met a new guy, I would ask her to prescreen them with her straightforwardness and unprecedented honesty. She herself met a good man, and they were together for eight years. I was very happy for her. Anastasia always cheered me up: "You deserve the best. You need a stronger man in your life. The man is supposed to pour you with flowers and expensive gifts. Don't be Mother Teresa. I know you are a very nice person. Remember, men are selfish and egoistic. You are beautiful, smart, and have a lot to offer. You should use studs for great sex and the rest of them for money."

Times have changed. Everyone is looking out for themselves. In a big city, you can't trust anyone. Three and a half years in New York City passed by quickly. Four Christmases, four New Year's Eves, and no boyfriend. I loved the top-notch landmark hotel brimming with celebrities and CEOs of Fortune 500 companies. But there is always that one person at work who ruins everything. There are nasty bastards all around us. In general, I did not hate anyone, but I could not stand my boss. He was very dramatic, impulsive, and unfair. He must had been a misogynist; he hated women at work—especially the smartest and most hardworking and lovable women. He saw women as his competition. We all hated him because he practiced favoritism. All of us were multilingual, passionate, and dedicated individuals. But he praised the incompetent, lazy, and careless ass-kissers.

What impressed me the most about New York City is its diversity of cultures, inexhaustible and contagious energy, fiercely competitive business environment, and much more. What I am taking with me are only the best moments, practices, and opportunities to become the best. All these amazing experiences enriched my life. Now it is time to change and explore all parts of the greatest USA. Change is a remarkable thing in life. If you are not happy, then make a change. Adrenaline was rushing through my head and body.

I moved to Miami, a city that welcomed me with widespread arms. The first night I arrived at the South Beach Hotel, I was impressed with its electrifying vibe, chic interior, and so many beautiful people. The weather in January was gorgeous. Just the thought of New York's weather made me realize I was falling in love with Miami.

I stayed for a little at my friend Lola's. She is a great friend with eternal optimism. Lola married a Cuban man, and they conceived three children within two years. It must be the result of a hot-blooded Cuban and Lola's positivity. Her husband is very sociable and easygoing. Only once did he make me feel uncomfortable: "Alexandra, you would be a great mother, and if you need a sperm donor, I can be the one."

My face turned red, and Lola giggled. I diplomatically declined his generous offer and responded in a soft voice, "I will find a more natural way of becoming a mother."

One day, I was sunbathing at the pool of my first brand-new apartment. The sunbeams were touching me; the crisp air hugging me, a little Cuba Libre buzz and Miami made me the happiest person in the world. A tall good-looking man approached me with a beer in his hands. His name was Oscar; he was wearing a see-through blue shirt. I found it funny and weird to see his nipples. He had big dark-brown eyes, a pointed nose, and beautiful teeth. We were chilling at the pool all day and drinking beer. Since that day, we were into each other and had never been apart. I was beyond excited—my first week in Miami, and I had already met the very attractive and laid-back Oscar.

Professionally, I got back into sales the same month. I was craving and so eager to get back into sales. I got a job offer on the spot in the first hotel I stepped in, in Miami. Finally, fortune was smiling at me. The chemistry with Oscar was instant. He had a sweet personality and a big heart. I was his love at first sight. Two months of dating flew by fast. He asked me to move in with him, but understandably, my parents did not approve me moving in with him unless he was going to marry me. I recall my mom telling me, "If you find a good guy and he loves you as much as you love him, hold on to him. You can mold him and make him a better man. The man is a head, and a woman is a neck. Head turns the same way neck does."

Six months since we met, he proposed to me at the same spot at the pool where we first laid eyes on each other. His family loved me. They were Americans but of Mexican descent. For some inexplicable reason, he was ashamed of being Mexican. I heard that Latin Americans perceive Mexicans in the USA as low-class. Despite Oscar's presumptions and shame of being Mexican, everything about him was perfect. The sex was amazing. The day he proposed to me, Oscar had included my name on his life insurance policy. The policy was for $250,000 if ever something were to happen to him. He was caring and loving, and he wanted to make me the happiest woman in the world. I felt lucky to have met Oscar. He loved me deeply. A week later, Oscar planned our celebratory engagement weekend in Key Largo. He knew that I love short getaways and traveling; I always enjoyed romantic dinners with Oscar.

One day, he told me, "Baby, I have to tell you something." His voice was trembling. "I had a vasectomy done three years ago. I love you so much. I do not want to lose you. If you want to have kids, I will get a vasectomy reversal."

I was shocked. Deep inside, I realized if a man does not want to have children, it will not end up well and it serves the recipe for a breakup. In his experience, the kids destroy the relationships. It is natural that I will love my children more than him. It was too late to break up because I was in love with him and he was crazy about me. The thought of not having him in my life scared me. Would I be happy again? Would it be the same? What if I do not find anyone who would love me more and as much as Oscar does? In love, we love ourselves; lucky is the one who loves the other person more in this love.

To make it work, I demanded he get the vasectomy reversal done. And Oscar kept his promise; he started actively looking for a doctor who would perform this procedure. He did not want to lose me. A few weeks later, he got vasectomy reversal done somewhere in Kansas. After his vasectomy reversal, I had never seen bigger and such dark-blue balls in my life. Sadly, Oscar had no friends to tell this embarrassment or share the good news. The fact was, Oscar had not even a single friend. I considered him a suspiciously introverted person.

Right after the vasectomy reversal surgery, we decided to hold our wedding in Uzbekistan with my family. I saved enough money for airline tickets and gifts for my entire family. Now I think I should have made him pay for everything. I do not get traditions here where the bride pays for the wedding with the consideration that the husband takes care of the family for the rest of their lives. But these days, we both need to be working; and therefore, both contribute to maintaining a lifestyle equally.

The wedding ceremony in Uzbekistan with my family was beautiful. Both parents always told me about how important it was to find a good human being in my life and to be respectful of each other and compromise. I thought, *Finally at thirty-two, I have found the love of my life.* Oscar made me happy, and I thought I would be the happiest when I become a mom. I was dying to have a son and a daughter—to love and care and raise them so that they could become good and happy children.

After we returned from Uzbekistan, something weird happened with Oscar. Weekends became the most anticipated days for him. He got wasted regularly. I thought he needed to get detached over weekends. I just did not want to lose that moment of euphoric and passionate love. They say that relationships, after a while, become a routine web, as the flame—the sparkle—fades away. We took a chance to save the relationship and work on it.

Months flew by, and we could not get pregnant. The oncologist said that vasectomy reversal had fifty-fifty chances of successful conception. I did the annual checkup, and my ob-gyn always told me to just keep trying.

In relationships, everything that starts well ends soon. We both needed to figure out how to make it work. Then I received heartbreaking news: Oscar had been taking an antidepressant, Zoloft, for the past eight years. I have my opinion about antidepressants, which I had expressed to Oscar: "I understand and sympathize, but I do not believe that the happy pills can cure you. You must take a control over this dependency."

Oscar was immensely stressed out because the antidepressant was causing impotence. When mixed, antidepressants and other stimulants have an adverse effect: misery, suicidal thoughts, and weakness. I tried to calm him down and set him for a positive mindset. But his weak ass started mixing Zoloft with alcohol. He got wasted and blacked out for three consecutive months. He would disappear in the middle of the night, and I had to look for him searching the streets. It was so embarrassing to find him in parks, on the streets, and on the ground next to a bus station. After seven months of humiliation, embarrassment, and abusive behavior, I decided to leave depressive, crybaby Oscar.

My imagination helps me solve problems and relax, and it brings me a promising, better future. So I began to imagine Oscar's sperms in action. I called Oscar's sperms *mariachi* to honor his Mexican heritage. I pictured these drunk and depressive mariachis dressed up in traditional attire and floating down the Miami River. In this metaphor, the Miami River clearly was my uterus. They were getting dehydrated, as they were inhaling alcohol every ten minutes:

"Lishten to me. Hey. The bartender can I have pleashhe?" It took him five minutes to pronounce her name. "Sh...Sha... SshhasShahShash. I want to make her hhhapppy."

One of the mariachis got up off his chair and raised his self-made Sprite bottle. The Sprite bottle had 70 percent of vodka and only 30 percent of Sprite. The cheap and depressive maniacs always dressed down in an undershirt and drank on the streets and by the pool holding a Sprite bottle. One of the most aggressive and bravest mariachis called Machoman yelled across the river at the rest of the 250,000 mariachis, "It has been three years since we left, and we are back, baby. It is great to be alive. Tonight is a big night for me! I am going to see my beautiful Alexandra. Drinks for everyone and more for me!"

So all post-vasectomy reversal or "oppressed" mariachis were free again, but they were slow and inefficient. Everyone shouted hooray and started dancing on the tables; one of them with biggest blue balls began to beat the shit out of the rest. Drunken fights are the best entertainment in many cultures. Most of them were dead, dehydrated, and blacked out. That night, not even Machoman mariachi made it, leaving the flower Alexandra very upset and disappointed. Well, a non-ambitious, oppressed, and depressed mariachi can't make her happy.

It was noon on a Tuesday. Oscar was still drunk and sleeping. I decided to wake his ass up and demanded an explanation. "What is wrong with you? What is happening, Oscar?"

Oscar had a guilty look and unbearably sad eyes. I had never seen him that bad. "My dad was diagnosed with cancer," Oscar said.

I immediately called his mom to ask her because I felt it was not true. His mom and I got along very well. My intuition had never let me down. His dad was all right. After I cornered him and demanded honesty, Oscar broke down and confessed, "Baby, I was unfaithful to you. I had sex with someone else." His voice was trembling, and he burst into tears.

At that moment, I felt like a huge knife stabbed me and made a hole in my heart. It was the first time I ever felt that way. "Why?" I looked at him, and suddenly I felt my legs shaking, and I burst out crying.

"You are perfect. Everything about you is perfect. I am not good enough for you. You are too much for me. I want to make you mine because you are strong and the best thing that could happen to me. I just want to do something crazy and stupid to test your love and convince myself that you love me as much as I love you." His puppy-like eyes were full of tears.

"This is the dumbest and most ridiculous shit I have ever heard. I don't understand," I said, feeling pain in my heart and crying. "You are mentally sick! I have no words to describe how heartbroken, embarrassed, and hurt I am."

All he cried back was, "I have a chemical imbalance. I have been taking antidepressants for years. It helps me, baby. Please understand me. You are not in Uzbekistan. You are in America. Medications can cure my depression."

Oscar was on a short-term disability leave, while I paid all the bills for three months. That was not upsetting to me. What was hugely disappointing to me was him making scenes, crying and crawling on the floor and asking for my forgiveness.

All those days, dark clouds hung over my heart, and I needed to work and get away from the depressing situation. His mom and sister flew in, and the whole Mexican drama got a kickoff. Oscar's first suicide attempt was to mix antidepressants and vodka. Oscar was taken to the hospital to clean up his stomach. He attempted two times to jump from the rooftop while screaming, drinking, and crying for seven hours and demanding that I do not leave him.

"You are my wife, Alexandra. You should stick with me at my worst. If you are leaving me, I will jump from the roof right now."

"If you were injured physically, I would take care of you and stay with you. But you have severe depression. You must be stronger, and you must promise me you will overcome it on your own. Do not blame me for your weaknesses and dependency."

Three shifts of Miami-Dade police officers advised me to get out of the relationship. After an exhausting seven hours standing on the rooftop in humid August and with humongous stress, I lost my patience. "Just jump off the roof. Please do all twenty police officers and me a favor. Just do it!" I screamed at Oscar.

Oscar's mom and sister pushed me so hard, and unexpectedly, I almost fell.

"You are going to kill my son. You are a Russian Asian bitch. I will put a curse on you!" his mom yelled.

It took seven hours, two suicide negotiators, and his physical exhaustion to get Oscar off the roof. There were social media fanatics who were trying to record the sad story. All this sequence of dramatic events made me realize Mexican telenovelas got nothing on him.

A day later, Oscar took my name off the life insurance and threw my clothes outside in boxes marked with my name. He was not mentally sick after all. He was not sick at all if the first thing he thought of was to take my name off life insurance and throw out my stuff. I didn't drop a tear when I was picking up my boxes. This low-life family and the depressive maniac would not see my tears. I am strong and very prideful.

Oscar and his entire family blamed me, love, and other drugs. It shocked me to the extent that I felt as if I had aged ten years. Oscar disappointed me big time. It was the right and smart move to end it right then and there than live with him and be miserable endlessly. Disappointment in a person is more painful than breaking up with someone you love. Antidepressants can't help anyone. Weak character, indecisiveness, and the inability to control your emotions are to blame.

I felt pitiful about Oscar; our love was over. Pitying a man does not make any relationship work. A few years later, someone saw him in the streets. He had lost everything and had become homeless. It was sad. He could not get out of it. A person with dependencies and without a strong willpower is a lost case. I wish him well genuinely.

Two years later, I had let it go. If I did not forgive Oscar, the anger and resentment would have eaten me inside out and caused insecurity and health issues. I want to be healthy and happy for the rest of my life.

Life goes on. I believe that I am solely responsible for my happiness and the choices I make. I will do my best to be happy again. I love myself more.

What not to date:

- A man with bad upbringing
- A man you didn't get to know better and take your time to get to know him
- A man with bad genetics and history of depressions
- A depressive maniac
- Someone with no friends
- Someone who wants to be with you 24-7. He does not give you enough space and privacy. He is like a sloth that hangs to you and attaches to you as a baby to a mommy.
- Someone with a feeble handshake
- Someone who does not have any hobby and outlets, does not like to work out, and is nothing but a couch potato

CHAPTER 2

50 First Dates

EVERY HOTEL SALESPERSON GETS EXCITED to attend travel shows hosted by major hotel brands. You get to enjoy lavish receptions with expensive steaks and lobsters. More importantly, you get to meet good-looking people, clients and sales managers or directors from other cities and properties. Entertaining top clients often ends up in a hotel room or partying until the wee hours of the morning. It's a win-win for all. You get to promote your brand, and it gets you a one-night stand with someone from a different city with no emotional involvement. What happens at the travel shows stays at the travel shows.

I attended a travel show in Baltimore, excited to meet new people and promote my hotel. The hotel company hosted a very nice cocktail reception for our clients, and dinner party was in full swing. A good-looking man who was smiling at me caught my attention. I just passed by and pinched his buttocks. He quickly turned around and grabbed my hand. "You are in trouble."

"What did I do? I have no idea what you are talking about."

"You just grabbed my ass."

Later, we ended up in my hotel room. He was good in bed, except for his turtleneck and his facial expression when he would come. He looked constipated. Well, out of all the problematic guys I dated, his funny orgasm expression was a minor defect. I could live with that. At least he had a career and came from a wealthy family. He loved writing me letters. How romantic and rare was that? Here was his first one:

Hi Alexandra,

I was sitting here thinking about you and thought I'd drop a line to start your day. Although it's only been a week, I enjoy our time together even if it's just on the phone and cannot wait to see you again. The more we talk, the more I find that we have many things in common. I hope the distance between us doesn't cause our interest in each other to fade. I can make more regular trips to see you. I wouldn't ask you to come up here…who the hell wants to go to Allentown?

I consider myself a very considerate and respectful man. Occasionally, I make comments about not intruding on your space when I came down in October. We've only known each other for a brief time, and I don't want you to think that you're stuck with me for the entire week. I want you to be able to tell me that you'd like some time to yourself or if you feel uncomfortable with my being with you for so long. I'm talking this to death but just want to respectful of your space. Feel free to tell me to shut up about it. I won't be insulted.

I have many aspirations in life and judge my success not by what I have, but what I've done and where I've been. I tend to like the finer things in life and would die if I had to live in the countryside. I like the city or sub-urban life where things are happening around me. I am a moderately conservative guy who is very social, confident and reliable. I am very friendly and try to see the positive side of things. I hate to use those clichés people use like "I see the glass as half full instead of half empty." Instead, I take a more creative approach and say I'd just get a smaller glass, fill it up and call it a day. I have never done drugs (never even smoked a cigarette) and have never dated a married woman. I find that utterly disgusting and self-destructive.

Naturally, I have my flaws, and I'm no choir boy. I am very competitive and hate to lose. When I was young, I was hit in the head playing football and have a poor memory. It can be frustrating for both of us and some-times is embarrassing for me. I do not trust people very easily (long and painful story), despise ignorance and disrespect.

I have attached some pictures. I'm sorry they're not as HOT as the ones you sent me. I don't look as good in cute panties as you do. One is a friend that I met while I was in Miami and the other is just after a 17-hour drive back from Florida (I look bad).

Have a beautiful day.

His picture looked good to me. I immediately sent his picture to Anastasia. She commented, "He is too simple for you. Something is off. His eyes are difficult to read, and I think you are going to be too much for him."

"I will date him long-distance and see where it takes us," I responded.

Aw. I received another letter from Tod:

Hi Alexandra,

Although I secretly hoped your plans had fallen through giving me an opportunity to see you again, I hope you had a great weekend with your friends in NYC.

Please forgive the email, but I wanted to write down my thoughts and see where I stood with you. Although it was over in an instant, I had a fantastic time. I had no idea you were going to be there AND how lovely you look and how much fun you are.

I moved many times throughout my career before finally returning to PA. My father owns an advertising agency, and it was my idea that I would learn the business and one day assume ownership. However, once someone gets to experience the excitement and enjoyment of our industry, it's too difficult to leave. Besides, I'd rather blaze my trails in life. That's why I moved back to PA.

I've decided that I cannot stay in the large metropolis of Allentown, PA and need to escape permanently. I'm at an interesting point in my career and will hopefully get a promotion as an Account Director within the next few months. If that happens, I may lock down a certain geographic location. It could be in Philly or on-site at the client's HQ (wherever that might be). There is a possibility that I can work remote, which would be ideal because I could live anywhere.

On the other hand, I may choose to sacrifice the upward advancement to live in an area that I wish and work remotely as a Travel Buyer. Miami, Dallas, Orlando & Jacksonville are a few of the cities I've been considering. I hate the cold!

I don't expect you to have any serious feelings for me or any expectations for us, but I wanted to find out where you are in your life. For right now, our time together is restricted, but I wanted to see if you would be interested in seeing more of each other.

I just had my vacation approved from 10/19–10/23 to "pay respects" to my 30's and am trying to figure out what to do or where to go. A friend of mine has a family-owned condo in Pompano Beach, and we've talked for months about going down there. I don't think he would be doing the entire week, but I have a lot of vacation to use.

Have an enjoyable day, Alexandra!

I wrote back:

Hi Tod,

I wish I had spent more time with you. Hopefully, we will catch up soon. Honestly, your E-mail made me smile a lot. I had indescribably fantastic time with you! I like you a lot. I will tell you on the phone about where I am in my life. Everything is fabulous in my life. I am interested in seeing you more. I understand you have a terrific opportunity with the company. You are at an interesting point indeed. I am so happy for you.

Why do not you come over to Miami? You can stay at my place. We will have an enjoyable time! I will plan according to whatever makes you happy.

Tod quickly replied:

Hello my dear,

Words alone cannot describe the weekend I had with you. The world looked completely different to me on my way home today. I had such a wonderful time with you that I felt compelled to write. During the flight, train ride and car ride home, I kept thinking of things I would write. Now that I have the keyboard in front of me, I can't think of what to say.

For many reasons, I'm not a person that allows my feelings to get out of control. I've seen friends and family members get destroyed by a spouse or significant other; I never wish to experience that. My emotions and feelings are the most important thing to me, and I guard them heavily. One very close friend of mine gave me a small figurine that reminded her of me. It's a little boy holding a big golden heart like a child would hold a favorite toy hoping no one would try to steal or break it. My friends and family know me as someone that will date someone briefly and back off completely. Previous girlfriends have said that I become very guarded when I get to a certain point in the relationship. It's not that I am incapable of love, I just feel that real love is much rarer than people are led to believe. So, if I begin to date someone and decide that this is not someone that I can love, my level of commitment only goes so far.

I hesitated to tell you about the man who ripped me off in California. Until then I felt that people were genuinely honest, and I had trusted freely. Now, confidence is much harder to gain. It wasn't the loss of money that hurt. Having someone violate your trust and take advantage of you publicly penetrated me much deeper than my checkbook. Now, when I meet someone who I care about, I am much more cautious.

I am excited about getting to know you and hope that we can continue to build a relationship together. My idea of a successful relationship is being best friends. I am so excited about all the things we plan on doing together.

> OK…I've sat in front of this keyboard for about an hour and forty minutes writing things and deleting them. I should just call you.

His openness and honesty touched me. Actions speak louder than words. I am cautious with men who talk a lot. Surprisingly, he was very consistent in calling me every night. We had fascinating conversations and joked over the phone.

October arrived. Tod flew to Miami for his vacation and birthday celebration. I picked him up at the airport with a surprise. It was boiling outside. He saw me wearing a trench coat and smiled at me. "What is up with the trench coat?" Tod asked.

I unbuttoned my red trench coat, and he saw me in red lingerie with gutter and fishnet stockings.

"Wow!" his jaw dropped. It was very original for a nerdy boyfriend. This nerd's facial expression was priceless. Tod was drooling with his mouth open.

For the next six days, we did a lot of fun stuff; we went to the beach, had sex every night, and more. I took him to meet my friend Lola and her husband. That evening, I cooked traditional Korean noodles with a Russian twist, which was Lola's favorite dish. We watched an interesting movie that was politically inclined with themes of corruption, war, Wall Street ripping off, and making billions stealing from people's life savings. He put the name of the movie in his Palm Pilot. He was still using a Blackberry.

Over dinner the next day, we spent hours talking about that movie and facts that were related to politics. A moment of awkwardness emerged when the waiter brought the check. Tension was in the air. I thought, *Why should I pay for it? He is staying for the entire week at my place, and I cooked dinner for him* *last night, and we are using my car. If he stayed at a hotel, he would have spent at least $1,500 in accommodations.*

I could read his mind, and he might be thinking, *Why wouldn't she offer to pay for dinner?* Tod slowly reached to get his wallet. I saw his eyes gazing at my hands. I looked away with my arms crossed.

The day before he left, I took him to a store. I had never asked a man to buy me stuff in my life. I decided to test him for the level of stinginess. Perhaps my Jewish girlfriend's strategy would work. Her strategy was to go to a trendy store a day prior to her date and make a list of clothes and shoes. She would make a reservation at a restaurant that was closer to the brand store, pick a dress and a pair of shoes, take it to the checkout line, and say in a very sexy tone through her nostrils, "Baby, I will wait for you outside. Would you take care of it and make your queen happy?" Her method worked all the time. I decided to try the same method.

"Baby, I like this dress and shoes. Do you like how it looks on me?" I gave him a sexy look.

He gave me a glazed look and said, "You have very expensive taste."

"If I had very expensive taste, I would have asked for Valentino or Gucci." I laughed. "Don't you remember you were going to buy me a gift before you leave?" I was shaking my boobs with a provocative look; my tongue was licking my upper lip in a sensual and slow way.

"I never promised you that." Tod got worked up.

"Yes, you did," I insisted with a warm smile.

Well, I ended up buying my dress and shoes. I felt very powerful and good about it.

The next day, he left for Allentown. I already knew it was not going to work out.

"I miss you, Alexandra. I showed your picture to my friends, and they don't believe me."

"What? Did you show them my pictures?"

"I am so lucky that I have got the sexiest, smartest, and most honest woman," Tod proudly said. "There is only one thing that bothers me. Can I ask you a question about it?"

"What is it? Shoot."

"I was telling my friends that I was paying for all dinners, and it made them think that you might have some financial difficulties. I meant to ask you all questions related to your financial and immigration status. Do you have a credit history? Do you have a lot of debts? Do you have a green card? Are you an American citizen? Tod was shooting all inappropriate questions like bullets from a Kalashnikov rifle for our two-month long-distance relationship.

"You talked about my financial situation and my citizenship status with your friends. I am upset now. By the way, I am an American citizen. My finances are none of your business, Tod."

"I think you are overreacting, Alexandra."

"By the way, you promised to buy me the dress and matching bag. But poor you, with your short-term memory, you do not have a recollection of it. Short-term memory loss is a bullcrap you made up. You were pretending to have a short-term memory out of convenience. You did not buy me flowers or a gift for hosting you. You should work on your manners and how to be a gentleman. When you stay at your friend's house, you are supposed to get a gift or at least flowers for a lady." I took revenge on him.

"Alexandra, I never asked you to contribute to my tickets. I was coming to see you. In a relationship, you contribute to my ticket if I am flying over to see you."

I hung up on him. He was very predictable; he kept calling me and asking me to send him his beach towel and beach shorts. I responded, "Since I have financial problems, you should give me your credit card, and I will be more than happy to send it via FedEx to your ass Express, which is three times more expensive and faster."

Tod continued to email, call, and ask me to work on the relationship. He would not remember to have good manners, but he would remember me not paying for dinner. Tod used his short-term memory loss conveniently. He had a good memory when it came to the dinner check and asking me to contribute to his airline tickets for visiting Miami.

What not to date:

- Pretentious men with short-term memory loss
- Ill-mannered men
- A man who does not bring you flowers on the first date
- A man who does not bring you a gift when he stays at your place
- A man with a turtleneck penis
- A man who discusses your financial situation with his friends
- A man whose friends are a bunch of douchebags
- A man whose facial expression of orgasm resembles constipation

CHAPTER 3

Bagels with Extra, Extra Cream Cheese

I PICKED ALL THE PIECES into one, shook it off, and felt relieved. It is the fact that I love myself more than anyone, and I want to keep it that way till I find someone who will win my heart over. I believe if you love yourself and know yourself best, you can make any man deserving of you happy and love him as much. One must have distinctive bones and a very strong core. I want someone who makes me better and wants me for the fact that I am a strong woman and a happy person. Happiness is a state of mind. Little cute things make me happy: the perfect sunny-side up eggs for breakfast, fresh-cut flowers, hearing the splash of waves, sharing meals with my friends, reading my favorite book for the third time, rediscovering myself, and aha moments.

The dating scene has changed dramatically. People rarely meet each other organically anymore. Nowadays, to find a reasonable and decent guy is a miracle. There is this saying: "Good guys are like good parking spots, always taken. Only ones for handicapped are left."

With all the dating apps, you have more options. But it should be about quality, not quantity. I have always been all about the natural way of meeting, but my single friends convinced me to sign up for online dating sites. It worked for some couples. The lucky ones fell in love, or they had bonded and proven that you never know, and it could work for me as well. So I decided to give it a try. I had nothing to lose.

All possible scenarios crossed my mind, and many other thoughts were running through my head. I could choose and pick whom I want, I could make all my unhappy married friends jealous, and finally, there could be good guys online as well. All the convincing signals and optimistic projections boosted my confidence. I was checking myself out in the mirror. I looked good. If I sucked in more air and wore spandex, my body was not in as bad shape as I thought. With never-ending enthusiasm, that same night I set up my profile, downloaded the best images of me, and voilà.

Tinder is a brilliant dating app. You shuffle through all profiles who are in the same geographic location. You set up your profile preferences, such as age and distance. I adapted to new digital platforms and e-dating.

One of my first matches was a British guy. His profile pictures were only of him lying down half-naked in bed with his hands behind his head. He had a look on his face that said, "I am clean, but I have a dirty mind." A minute later, I got a message via the Tinder app: "You are so beautiful. I can't wait to meet you in person."

"Thank you. You are good-looking as well. Let us meet up and see if we click."

"Sounds good. See you at Japanese Sushi Bar. 7:00 p.m." His British accent and husky voice made him even more desirable and hotter.

I am not going to lie, I was very excited, as it was my first e-date. I had put on my lucky black dress and red heels. I know there is a rule that a lady should get to the date place fifteen minutes later to keep the guy waiting, nervous, and excited. But I always get to the place on time. I felt good about the way I look. My black hair, red lipstick, and smoky eyes made me look mysterious.

It was 7:17 p.m. *Where is he? I will wait for five more minutes then leave.* I was just about to call my friend and tell her that he stood me up. It had happened to me in the past when I got stood up by jerks. Nothing new. But then there he was: tall, blue-eyed, clean-shaven, bold, and just flew in. And he gave me a very juicy kiss on the lips. Kissing with Richard did not embarrass me. I liked his strong expression of his affection for me.

"Hello, gorgeous! I was afraid you would not look as good as you did in the pictures. Wow! You are stunning," Richard said.

Lychee martinis were pouring in and all warming me up inside, and our lips met and indulged into passionate kisses all over again. I was getting butterflies. It was a feeling I had not had for a long time.

"Let us do shots. Have you ever drank sambuca?" said Richard in his sexy voice.

"No, never. I can't wait to try it."

"Two shots of sambuca, please!"

I took a sambuca shot, and instantly the entire portion of sambuca came out of my nostrils like a two-hole fountain. Richard and I burst into a loud laughter, while everyone at the bar turned around and looked at us with a judgmental look and a few genuine smiles. It was the funniest moment of our first date. I have no idea what exactly happened. But he and I burst into a thunderous laugh. Richard grabbed a napkin and wiped off all the sneezed-out sambuca from my nose. I can't deny it was the cutest moment. He was such a gentleman and was so chill about slightly embarrassing moments.

"Do you want to get out of here?"

A few minutes later, we had made out everywhere. He was such a passionate kisser. He pushed me against the wall, lifted my arms, and locked them with his steady right hand. His left hand was under my dress, touching and rubbing my thighs. He was kissing me from neck to shoulders, and he went down on me. I had been turned on in a garage. Someone could walk in any moment. The excitement took me over, and I felt very aroused by Richard.

"You are gorgeous. I have always wanted to date Asian women. I can't imagine life without you. You are exactly the way I have pictured you—silky hair, exotic look, firm ass, tight skin, and most importantly, you have a great personality."

I smiled at him and said flirtatiously, "You have exquisite taste."

I couldn't wait to see his package. Looking at his body proportion, hands, feet, it could be the right size and shape. Later that same night, we were in his air mattress, a very bouncy one. How romantic it was! Sambuca sprinkled out of my nose, air mattress, and no air-conditioning in a hot room. There was a bike in his room. Weird. Why would he keep his bike inside? His place was filthy, but he possessed the most expensive bike.

"I am a professional cyclist," he said. That explained why he had very firm calves. He was a cook by profession, ambitious, a professional cyclist, had an ironic sense of humor, and a future homeowner. After all the losers I dated, it felt like hitting the jackpot.

"I do not like convertible cars. They are ugly and incomplete. I would never get a convertible," said Richard.

"I love convertibles. It is so romantic to drive in my car. Everyone has a different opinion about everything else." I did not get resentful. Everyone has different tastes.

We were celebrating one week since we met. Like Russians say, "If there is an occasion, vodka is always available."

He said, "I can't imagine life without you." Richard caressed my body, kissing me from head to toe. His fingers brushed through my hair. The entire foreplay turned me on. But his boy was soft and felt like a gummy bear. Richard looked very frustrated. "Wait. Give me twenty minutes, baby. Go down on me. It's never happened before." His husky voice and British accent were such a turn-on for me. He must had been very nervous and super excited. "Just kiss me and caress me, baby." I tried to be understanding.

A few hours later, his boy was still very soft like a chewy gummy bear. We tried various positions—doggy style, missionary, sideways—but nothing worked. I thought it would work next time I'd see him. I was such an optimistic gal.

I spent almost every other night at his place. In the middle of one night, I was thirsty, and I got up for a glass of water. I turned the lights on, and when I saw cockroaches dancing on the tables, I screamed. At that moment, two other roommates of this forty-six-year-old man jumped out of their rooms. His roommates were half-naked and unemployed. The way I see it, your house reflects your personality, taste, and organizational skills.

He found out that his roommates were fooling him and getting money from him. The place was a foreclosure before Richard moved in. The owner of the apartment moved back to Colombia, put his nephew and girlfriend in the apartment, and made Richard pay the entire rent. So they were living for free, and he had no idea. As a matter of fact, foreclosures were springing up like mushrooms after the rain in Miami in 2009–2011 after the housing bubble.

But at that moment, all I was thinking was how long it would take him to get it up. I wanted sex. *Please satisfy me, Richard.* He went down on me, but I wanted him inside me.

Hours passed by. I got disappointed again, as his gummy bear kept slipping away. I just needed to catch it, squeeze it, and push it inside. I was doing my best to make it hard, but every time it got a little harder, it slid back in and went down within a few minutes.

"You are my soulmate," said Richard. "After what you went through with your ex-fiancé, we will heal together. We will merge into one soul."

I had never had anyone say such words that touched my heartstrings.

Days flew by. We enjoyed each other's company, but when it came to sex, he could not get it up. There must be a solution or treatment to make our relationship work.

Then I received good news. Richard asked me to go house hunting, as he wanted me to move in with him. All my girl-friends went crazy. They were all jealous and told me, "You are a lucky one. Just three weeks in, first Tinder date, and you are moving in with your boyfriend into a new house. Lucky bitch. We are happy for you."

A few female friends will be genuinely happy for you. Love me or hate me, I am still going to shine. People get jealous because they are insecure and unhappy.

When we met, I was actively looking for another job. It is true for me that job stability affects my relationships positively. I felt like the luckiest girl in the world. I had a fantastic job offer, confidence, and a boyfriend with a new house but with erectile dysfunction. Hopefully it could be fixed. Every problem has a solution.

"Congrats on the new job, gorgeous!" Richard told me over the phone.

"It calls for a celebration! I love my life!"

"Sure it does. I will pick you up at seven p.m. I can't wait to see you, gorgeous."

I was counting down the minutes. Tonight would be the night to get down. Around 6:30 p.m., my phone rang, and I heard him say, "I can't make it, and sorry for letting you down.

I got so much going on now. Unfortunately, we can't see each other because I am dying of cancer. I am sick and tired of Miami and its shallow people. That is why I am moving back to England."

"What? Just two days ago, you were in love with Miami and me. I do not believe you." My voice sounded disappointed.

"Believe me, I hate Miami. Miami has the worst people in the world." Richard did not sound convincing.

"I love Miami, and I am fortunate to have met great people and made wonderful friends. This is bullcrap. Something is wrong. My gut feeling tells me you are full of shit."

I drove to his house but could not find him. I kept calling him, but he did not pick up his phone. I told my friends about Richard, and none of them could believe how stupidly and cowardly he had broken up with me. Two hours later, Richard texted me back, saying, "I think you got the wrong number. My name is Kaitlyn."

My friend Olga and I burst into a thunderous laugh the moment we heard his lame response. We got creative; we copied and pasted Richard's face instead of Bruce Jenner's and sent it to Richard. How timely and appropriate! It was the day when media outlets published Bruce Jenner's transformation into a woman. Richard got so mad at me and was cursing in his bloody plummy accent.

On an ever-beautiful Miami day, I was driving to work in my cute convertible with the top down; and in the corner of my right eye, I saw Richard cycling very fiercely. He looked like he beat cancer—nasty bastard, liar, and pitiful pig. How convenient that I had a bucket of freshly baked Einstein bagels. I couldn't wait to throw those creamy and freshly baked bagels at his pathetic face—not at him, but through him. The traffic was bumper to bumper. It was the perfect setting. As I was getting closer, my excitement to kick his ass was exhilarating.

"You have resurrected, asshole? Do you want a bagel? How do you like your bagels? You look like you love your bagels with extra, extra cream cheese!"

I spread cream cheese generously on a garlic bagel and threw the bagel with extra, extra cream cheese on his pale face. He lost control and fell off a $2,000 bike. His face looked like a white wall, and his lips were trembling. At that moment, I burst out laughing. It was a very powerful and evil laugh. Miami is a small city, and his "cooked balls" were not curable. It must be so frustrating for Richard to not be able to get it up. Apparently, the reason behind cooked balls is because regular and constant cycling raises the temperature. The heat and movement could result into cooked balls.

There is a joke in Russia about impotence. A professor in medical school was asking a question, "What do you call a man who wants to have sex but can't get it up?"

A stunning girl raised her hand and answered, "The man is called impotent."

"Correct. What do you call a strongly hung man who does not want to have sex with you?"

There was a long pause and puzzled faces. A chubby, big-boned, and highly enthusiastic female raised her hand and shouted out, "He is a moron!"

Everyone burst into thunderous laughter.

What not to date:

- Men who tell you they are crazy about you on the second date
- Men who have issues getting it up all the time
- Men whose place is filthy
- Men who lie about cancer and use it as a reason to break up

- Men who can't satisfy any woman. No woman in this entire world would want a man with this problem. Huge problem.

Next! Moving on!

CHAPTER 4

Obvious

SINCE I AM A VERY optimistic gal, I decided to try a different online dating site. The new dating site requires you to fill out your profile. It does take a considerable amount of time to describe yourself in the best light possible. Everyone writes good things about themselves—how great, funny, intelligent, and good they are, which are 95 percent untrue. Luckily, I came across a fascinating profile. An aerospace engineer wanted a family and kids. He was a homeowner; he was positive, tall, good-looking, and intelligent. He was good on paper. We spent hours on the phone talking about everything and everyone, even politics and religion. We all know these two subjects are very sensitive. Surprisingly, I felt very comfortable talking about anything with Alex.

"Are you religious, Alexandra?" he asked curiously.

"No, I am an atheist. I can't say that I am spiritual either. These days, quite a few people call themselves spiritual to make a better impression on others. I have my moral principles such as be respectful, use your common sense, be the best at what you do, and be an honest, loyal, and good human being. It scares people off and gives them the opportunity to judge atheists. From my experience, fanatic religious people are judgmental, hypocrites, and shady."

"Well-said. I concur. Great. I have the same opinion about super religious people," said Alex in his calm and chill voice. "Do you like George Carlin and Bill Maher?" Alex asked.

"I love both. Maybe we can watch stand-up comedy on TV together."

"We are going to make such a good couple, Alexandra. We are smart, and we could be a good team. Would you like to go out for dinner?" asked Alex with hope in his voice.

"Dinner would be perfect." I smiled over the phone.

"How about this Saturday? Eight p.m.?"

Alex was good-looking, tall, and intelligent; and he had a profound sense of humor. He sounded amazing. I was flying around the house and getting ready for my date. I put my emerald-green bandage dress. I felt very confident he was completely going to love the look. The dress looked so good with my black hair. We had agreed to meet at the restaurant. I got there a little bit earlier and headed to the bar to relax before my date showed up. It is always good to loosen up beforehand because you don't know how it might go down or how disastrous a night can turn.

The restaurant was a very romantic restaurant, lit up with candles all over. I was surprised that Alex had good taste. I guess never underestimate anyone you do not know. The restaurant manager was very good-looking. While I sipped my cosmopolitan cocktail, I glanced up at the wine connoisseur's body wrapped in a bustier with fishnet stockings. She was climbing a rope to get the most expensive wine. In my mind's eyes, Alex was tall, handsome, and well-dressed. I couldn't wait to meet him in person.

A few minutes later, I felt a touch and light tap on my shoulder. I turned around in slow motion; my smile faded faster than the speed of light. My date turned out to be a four eight, short, and skinny guy. He looked like a ten-year-old boy. I recognized his pleasant voice, and I glanced at the smallest hands I had ever seen in my life. He was wearing a tight dress shirt with suspenders. *Why would he wear suspenders? If he had a long torso, that would look good on him. Somebody please get me out of here!*

"You look prettier in person, Alexandra," said Alex in his soft and calm voice.

I couldn't say the same thing about him. I sighed disappointingly. How could Alex be so stupid? Your height is the first physical attribute that is visible, and it's an obvious fact. I always date tall guys. And the tallest guy I had dated was six five. I tried breathing in and out, containing myself, and I pretended that I liked him at least for an hour.

"It is nice to meet you, Alexandra." His eyes were shining.

"Shall we order the food? I am starving," I asked him in a slightly irritated tone.

"Yes, I am hungry as well."

"Do you like bacon? I see bacon-wrapped dates stuffed with chorizo on the menu."

"No, I do not eat bacon," Alex said in a firm voice.

"That surprises me, as Cubans love pork," I stated, a puzzled tone in my voice.

"I am not one of those Cubans."

Meanwhile, I kept staring at the hottest Italian man I had ever seen in my life—a good-looking man covered with olive skin and veiny hands, neck, and something else. Visible veins are a sign of male health.

"Alexandra, before you go to the ladies' room, can I kiss your hand?"

The tables were broad and tall, so he had to get on the chair, climb, stretch half his body, and reach out and kiss my hand. His face was the size of my fist. Everything was so small on him: face, body, legs, hands, and feet. "Alexandra, I like you, and I think we make a good team. You are making good money, and so am I." Alex was continuously happy. *I just can't date shorter guys than me. I am short. What am I going to do now? I can't just leave now. I will not be a good girl. I can't give up on yummy risotto and decadent and good wine. I can't wait to taste the dessert menu. I just love food! I hope this is the last time I am taller than my date. Imagine how I would look in bed spooning with a tiny guy. We'd look like small kids. Is his penis in equal proportion to his height? It will not get to that point.*

"Dessert now or later at my place?" Alex asked me with the biggest smile on his tiny face.

"I am craving for a chocolate mousse with vanilla ice cream here and now, please."

The chocolate mousse with vanilla ice cream was something to die for! It was delicious, frothy, and creamy—the best decadent mousse ever! I dropped a spoon by accident and rushed to pick it up. Here was the truth: I saw his shoes with heels under the table. And my eyebrows went over my head when I saw his legs were hanging in the air and did not even touch the floor. I pushed his shoes under his chair so that when he couldn't find them, I could see his real height. Those shoes were Pierre Cardin Cuban with built-in heels. I googled using words such as *Cuban, men's shoes, built-in heels.* It is amazing how Google works. If you type related words to the product or service you are looking for, you get the relevant information. I wish the same rule would apply to online profiles on dating websites. The guys should be honest about physical attributes, especially their height. It is evident.

The truth is, everyone wants to be loved and to love somebody—all types: short, ugly, goofy, stupid, fat, and obnoxious. I have not talked to him since. I do not have any desire to see his face and feet on the heels.

What not to date:

- Someone who posts all pictures of his face with sunglasses on
- Someone who does not eat bacon
- Someone who is stupid and smart at the same time
- Someone who lies about his height by posting pictures of his face only in sunglasses (when what-not-to-date signs are unavailable because of a false picture or height)

CHAPTER 5

Stingy Bastard

IT WAS GIRLS' NIGHT OUT, and my good friend Carolina and I were meeting up with her crazy party animals at Blue Martini Brickell. Brickell is the Wall Street of the South. The spot attracts all businessmen and tourists as well. What men in Brickell lack is the confident walk with swagger.

"To us, friendship, and love!" I toasted and raised my cocktail.

"Hey, *Chinita*, a guy is checking you out. Do not turn around now. Do it slowly."

"He is all right. Nothing special."

Ten minutes later, the guy across the bar was cheering and sending us drinks. He approached me, and we were flowing into a pleasant conversation. His name was JB, and he worked for a morgue. Later that week, he invited me for dinner. He was not my type. He was a little bit chubby, and he had a huge black mole above his lips. I decided to give it a try. JB made a reservation at the newest and nicest restaurant in the upcoming area of Miami. It would be great if JB was more attractive.

The preconceived notion of attractiveness made me attract wrong guys. Good-looking guys I dated turned out to be jerks and egoists. At the end of the day, beauty fades away with years;

great personality and interesting conversations are the only luxuries that we are left with.

"Thank you for making tonight a beautiful night."

"Aw, my pleasure."

"What would you like to drink? Cocktail or wine?"

"Bloody Mary for Me, please."

"How about you?"

"Water. Still water. I am your designated driver tonight, Alexandra."

"It means more for me." I burst out laughing.

"Are you ready to order?" a good-looking waiter asked us.

"Yes, oysters to start. For entrée, branzino with cherry tomatoes and olives."

"Excellent choice, young lady."

"Soup of the day and chicken sandwich. If it is too big and I do not finish it, I would need a box to go," JB said.

"Unfortunately, we do not have the chicken sandwich for dinner, sir," the hot waiter responded with a puzzled look on his face.

"I am not that hungry," JB stated with an uncertain tone.

The entire evening, we carried an interesting conversation, but I did not find him attractive. There was no chemistry. He was scooping out the last drop of the soup from the smallest cup I had ever seen. *I should stop overthinking too much.*

"Are you done with your soup?" the waiter asked patiently.

"No, I am still working on it."

"Isn't the service excellent here?" I commented.

"The service is bad. They just want to take your dishes away so fast. I am not done yet," JB said in a grumpy voice.

"I can't wait to taste branzino with cherry tomatoes and olives." I was drooling.

Branzino was one of the most expensive entrées on the menu. *Hopefully, my expensive taste would scare him, and he will not call me anymore.*

"I always order what I can finish eating. There are so many kids out there who are hungry."

"It is sad. I want bread pudding for dessert," I responded. I was trying to do something stupid so that he would not like me. Every minute, I was getting annoyed with his stupid and irrelevant statements. I wanted to just eat the yummy dinner and go home, counting the minutes to get out of there.

"Do you want to go to the lounge close by? We can grab a drink and dance." I just could not find a reason not to go because he asked me so suddenly. We headed out to a lounge, and the moment we got in, he excused himself and disappeared for a good fifteen minutes.

"Where have you been?" I was very much annoyed.

"I was trying to locate the owner of the club."

"What for?"

"Well, I wanted to flash my Miami-Dade Police badge and get free drinks. I am trying to save every buck anywhere and every time I can."

I excused myself and flew out of the club like a bullet.

I can't date stingy guys. It is just such a turn-off. Some girls are cheap too. There was a friend of mine. She always ordered the most expensive entrée and drank the most cocktails, but when the check arrived, she was the first to scream and suggest, "We should split it equally and evenly. Aren't we all friends and cool with it?"

If they find each other, it'd be a perfect match. I would call them a practical couple. There is absolutely nothing wrong with it. Everyone finds his or her better half.

What not to date:

- Someone who is stingy
- Someone who uses the line "There are a lot of hungry kids out there. I always finish my food and take a doggy bag"
- Men who use their police badges to get free or heavily discounted drinks and food when they are on a date

CHAPTER 6

Curiosity Satisfied

IT WAS A SIZZLING SUMMER night. The day was sinking into darkness. I was walking down the street after a long stressful day at work. There were food trucks, amateur art pieces, and a bunch of cute guys. I was looking at one of the sculptures. There are two kinds of artists: gifted and amateur. Amateur artists express their vision and life perspective through art, but they lack the gift and need to get an education. Art requires finesse, precision, and extraordinary creativity.

Suddenly, I heard a low-pitched voice of an African American man. I was always curious as to why male African Americans have a distinct voice.

"Do you like this sculpture?"

"Not really."

"I am Terrence. And this is my friend, Jack. He is an artist at our financial company, and he has his studio at the office."

Terrence was a tall and big African American mixed with French. I always heard, "Once you go black, you never go back." But I had never been attracted to them. Curiosity is the best way to learn and experience something for the first time. There is always a first time for everything.

"That is very cool. I am Alexandra."

"How are you doing tonight?"

"Fantastic."

"I would love to invite you to dinner, Alexandra."

I hesitated for a second but asked him to give me his number.

That same night, his boss took everyone out for drinks, and Terrence invited me along. It was a very fun night at a local dive bar in South Beach. A few days later, we went out for drinks at a strip club. I heard it was the dream of every guy to have a cool girlfriend to go to a strip club with and get a lap dance. Anyway, the strip club did not have what I had not seen.

I just wanted to kill my curiosity about black guys and give a stamp of approval or stamp of denial for myself. I guess it is true that once you go black, you never go back. The way Terrence loved me in bed got me screaming. His body was kind of heavy and with stretch marks he called tiger stripes.

I prefer sex with slim guys. Slim and fit guys look better and do it with finesse or better, for lack of a better word. Big muscular guys and overweight men do not have finesse. They just throw their bodies on you, and you can't even breathe. I recall having a one-night stand with a big muscular white guy. To my biggest surprise, the white boy wanted to be black—a rapper. I called him Failure to Become Eminem. He was listening to rap music only, talking like black people, drinking Hennessey, using slang, and walking with a swag—especially when he saw an attractive black woman. I find it amusing when people want to be someone else. Sadly, he had a teenier meaner short wiener, and worst of all, he was a put-'n'-shoot. I guess all the muscles were proportionally distributed all over his body but skipped the meat popsicle of the big muscle guy. How deceitful looks can be!

"It is so refreshing to meet a smart, independent, and sexy woman these days," Terrence said in his gospel voice. "Well, the first thought that had crossed my mind, dear, was when I saw those beautiful legs, I knew there must be an interesting story hidden. You are like a unicorn. Asian with a black woman's ass. Your skin is sugar-honey roasted. It looks like it and tastes like it. I want to call you *Adjion!*" (pronounced as ei-djon).

"Why?" I giggled like a brook flowing merrily through a well-lit wood.

"It sounds more sophisticated," added Terrence.

Three months passed by, and most of the time, he stayed at my place. Our sex life was a sex escapade: sex in the bathtub, in the ocean, standing up on my high heels, every night and lunch breaks. Amazingly, his big boy would never go down. It was like a towel rack, ninety degrees up all the time. It was a perfect angle, never bent over and falling to either side. Another huge plus: Terrence turned out to be a great cook. He would cook French onion soup, calzone, chicken cordon bleu, to name a few. Everything Terrence cooked was sumptuous and tasty.

I think we all should learn how to cook at an early age. I remember my mom teaching me how to cook Korean and Russian food when I was a teenager. My mom did not let me go out and hang out with my friends till I learned cooking. It comes in handy for both men and women. Terrence and I shared good stories about our moms' cooking. The best recipe of moms' cooking is love, soul, right proportion, and spices. Honestly, I was impressed with his cooking skills.

I guess amazing sex, cooking skills, nightly massages, and fun personality compensate for an average intellectual level. You can't find a perfect man. The perfect man does not exist.

"How come you never dated a black guy before?" Terrence asked me.

"I have not been attracted to black men. I find them as lazy guys, and I heard that most of black men are horndogs."

"Ouch, that hurts. I will prove to you we are not lazy, and I am a one-woman man."

Since that night, he would cook and clean my place and would give me an orgasmic foot massage every night. He had a good heart and splendid sense of humor.

In a blink of an eye, Christmas was around the corner. Terrence took me shopping. He got a baby-pink skirt with a matching blouse for me. I could not decide on what to wear for an office holiday party.

"Do you want me to go Kanye West on Kim with you?"

"I would say yes, but you are not Kanye." I burst out laughing, as it was the cheesiest thing he ever told me.

I love the anticipation of New Year: new beginnings, new people at work, and new excitement. The office Christmas party was in full swing. The champagne was pouring in, house and techno music was jamming, and everyone was having a fun time. Everyone was complimenting us: "You are a very vibrant couple—Asian and Black!" The night ended with amazing sex.

"Do you want to have kids?" Terrence asked me suddenly.

"Yes, I wanted them, but I am in my early forties. I am not sure if it is still possible."

"Well, my soldiers are still marching."

I could not tell him that I did not want to have a baby with him. Instead I was laughing so hard because I was imagining African soldiers marching and myself, dressed as the North Korean leader in charge of everything. I was holding a whip, and as soon as I saw the soldiers marching, I beat them hard, and they backed off.

"Do you have regrets about your relationships that did not work out?"

"Right now, that is a very personal question. We do not know each other so well, and I don't feel comfortable talking about it."

"Is my expiration date approaching?"

"What do you mean, Terrence?"

"Well, every guy has an expiration date. You have a set time when you break up with your boyfriend."

"It did not cross my mind yet."

"So do you regret losing that perfect guy?" he asked me with anticipation in his voice that I was going to say I don't.

But to throw back at him, I responded, "Yes, he was the one I wanted to be with. But he did not want to have any more kids. Well, now, six years later, he knocked up someone and married her. It could have been me. He is the CEO of a high-tech company. He is a good person and is successful. The chemistry was electrifying. We enjoyed traveling, fine dining, having conversations about politics, and we are both atheists. We are both multilingual, and we had the same dream: to open a small vineyard and bed-and-breakfast in Tuscany. I was so happy with him."

"Well, I took a three-month computer class, and I bet I can do what that CEO does." His voice sounded like a competitive horse.

I laughed in response and said, "How can you compare your basic course to a master's degree in IT and founder of a high-tech company?" I was irritated with his immaturity. I rolled my eyes; it really bothered him that I still regretted not fighting for a great guy. "Do you have any regrets, Terrence?" I threw right back at him.

"When I was a pimp, I treated women badly."

"I am in shock. That is wrong. How could you treat women so badly?"

I felt disgusted, and that was the moment I decided to break up with him. I always know and am very decisive on kicking out and breaking up with a bad guy.

"Did you sleep with your prostitutes?" I asked him with disappointment in my voice.

"I do not waste my dick," said Terrence, and he looked like he thought he was very smart by making that statement.

Four months passed by, and like Russians says, "Chocolate-and-flowers season is off." The reality check hit hard. I held him responsible for bills. I started to ask Terrence for help with the bills, as he lived at my place all the time. I didn't like his place, as it did not have a good vibe. He lived with his aunt who paid all the bills.

"I do not inherit anyone's debt," he replied in an angry voice.

"What does it have to do with it?" I was getting furious.

"Your place, you pay for it."

Anger took over me, and I yelled at him, "You know, then leave my place. Get out. Pick your shit up and get out of my house now!"

"Can we talk about it? I am your friend. Can we at least talk as friends?"

"No, get out of my house. Now."

I dropped him off because he never had a car. I felt bad.

There were other moments and other reasons when and why I decided to break up with him for good. The worst thing about Terrence that I found out was that he abandoned his daughter when she was two years old. To me and millions of parents out there, it was cruel of him to leave his child. All kids want is love, care, and attention. She had been missing her father. His ex-wife sent their daughter to Miami. I used to kick him out to make him devote time to his child. Terrence wanted to spend more time with me than with his daughter. I used to tell him, "You can find as many women as you want. But that you deliberately avoid spending time with your own child is inhumane. Even most animals in this world take care of their babies and sacrifice their own lives to feed and care for their own babies."

At work, it was the worst time for me. I got fired for the first time by the heartless general manager who liked ass-kissing. He was Surinamese. I got fired because he did not like my straightforwardness. The fact that I was standing up for my team drove him crazy and hurt his ego deeply. Sadly, when a new hotel management company takes over, they "clean house." I know for a fact that some takeovers are hostile and they happen overnight. People come to work only to be told on the spot that they have no jobs. I called him Ruthless Fraud. He fired the entire team of hardworking and loyal people who had worked for that hotel for twenty years. Ruthless Fraud blamed everyone in the team when something went wrong, but Ruthless Fraud always wanted to take credit when the hotel achieved greater financial results and received five-star reviews from Tripadvisor.

In my opinion, Tripadvisor and Yelp reviews are not 100 percent unbiased. The hotels and restaurants are compared to inadequately competitive hotels. The online reputation, abundance of five-star reviews, and specials or promos dictate their positioning and ranking on search engines and booking sites. As a matter of fact, low demand and unreasonable comparison disrupt the pricing strategies, resulting in price wars and leaving the customers with fewer choices. There are a few reputable management companies that even buy five-star reviews and hire people in India and China to write reviews about the businesses. From my recent experience, the companies that buy five-star reviews have the worst customer service.

It is a vicious act to fire staff who are in their late fifties and older. It is harder to find a job at that age. The hard truth is, it is easier for young people in this country to land a job. Ruthless Fraud was acutely aware of this but still decided to fire them. Selfishly, Ruthless Fraud called himself a leader. I should clarify the definition of a great leader in my own words. Leaders are people persons who positively impact every single employee, support everyone with the right tools and resources, and give due credit to the team.

I wonder if wives and husbands or girlfriends and boy-friends of Ruthless Frauds and Snitch Bitches cuddle and sleep in the same bed for many years. There are Ruthless Frauds all around us. We just do not see it under the mask of skillful pretentiousness.

In the eyes of the deluded owners, Ruthless Fraud made the best general manager because he made them money and made them richer. In fact, it was not true. Ruthless Fraud understaffed and cut salary by demoting and promoting with-out extra or equal pay. Ruthless Fraud promoted staff members at the same pay rate as if he did a favor. It was an insult to intelligence. Understaffing and underpaying the staff is not a proof and factor of successful hotel management or any busi-ness management. It is only a method to buy time. To prove a point and support the team, I criticized his wrongful actions in an email. It was sent out to all the managers and hotel owners. My email made everyone's day and made Ruthless Fraud furi-ous and run around the hotel asking each manager not to read my email. I felt great and proud of what I did; I spoke the truth.

There is a second type of rotten character that exists at every company called Snitch Bitches. They are even worse than Ruthless Frauds. Snitch Bitches get all the secrets and blab about the staff, gain the trust of the staff, and help Ruthless Frauds with firing. This Snitch Bitch was smart but insecure and did not get enough sex. Lack of sex makes them very ner-vous and jealous of others' success. I noticed most of them are unattractive and fat or skinny and unpleasant looking. There is something in their eyes. Eyes never tell a lie.

Very soon, Ruthless Frauds and Snitch Bitches will be erased from businesses and companies. The true colors of every person come out in a process of hardest problem-solving and decision-making. The decision must be rational, fair, and hon-est. Ruthless Frauds and Snitch Bitches always float like the biggest piece of shit on the surface of waters. Shit does not sink in waters.

On an optimistic note, I felt very relieved and motivated to pursue the best opportunity. I learned and moved on. Nothing brings me down or discourages me. My core is made of steel.

I had learned about another type of Ruthless Frauds through Terrence's work. The owner of the private lending company was a foreigner who had private investors mainly in shark loans. I called it BS funding.com. Invoice funding is the same entrapment as a credit card company. The BS funding makes money on interest rates that are outrageous—between 30–60 percent, depending on your credit history.

The famous quote by Honore de Balzac says it best: "Behind every great fortune lies great crime." All the financial scandals always reveal the main characteristics of the scammers: greedy, very persuasive, always have an answer that may sound reasonable to you, good-looking, attractive, and self-loving. What shocked me was the atrocious people whom the owner of the BS funding regularly hired. The entire office was highly testosterone-infused. The brokers were bullying new hires. It was full of no-class girls—nothing but huge boobs popping out, red hair, and legs with knee-high boots in the middle of humid summer in Miami. The entire company reminded me of a mediocre *The Wolf of Wall Street*.

The owner of BS funding.com hired desperate people and paid them $200 a week but promised big commissions to all his brokers. Among the employees, there were toothless, weird-looking, and mentally unstable drug addicts; depressive, manic lawyers; and people with criminal histories. His strategy was to use people, manipulate them, and make them loyal. They looked up to him because he "saved" and gave them a lifetime opportunity to become rich. All ruthless and toothless employees would bring trashy girls and have sex in their bathrooms and, after work hours, in dive bars, houses, and high-end strip clubs with cocaine and other drugs.

The way the business works is they fund small businesses and the invoices are at very high percentages. The merchants do not even realize that the business concept is entrapping them into bigger debts. The funding companies are making billions by throwing sand into their eyes and stealing the marketing database. There are a few invoice-based funding companies that blow up and make billions. The companies fix cash flow by advancing payments for outstanding invoices. But remember, the merchants must pay the BS funding.com at higher interests.

The most interesting character was the owner of BS funding.com called Foreigner Boner. He had European and Jewish background. One of his mistresses, called Jersey Shore, was his coworker. She was stupidly jealous, and she tried to break up with a married man because she discovered he had been sleeping around with another fifteen women—Dominican, Asian, Black, Italian, Scandinavian, the representatives of United Nations. Oh boy, he got around. How could you be jealous over a married boyfriend?

His mistresses were dumb if they believed that he was going to leave his wife and lose millions and split 50 percent of his wealth. His wife probably suspected him of cheating, but she kept quiet because she had financial security. In general, women stay in relationships even though husbands are cheaters and bad people. The fear of being alone takes over them, and the fear of losing access to all the money and luxurious lifestyles is too painful.

It was obvious that Foreigner Boner took care of himself and loved himself. He drove a Lamborghini, got a body massage religiously, dined only at five-star restaurants, and dressed only in trendy brand-name clothing. To make sure his wife and his mistresses would not suspect him of infidelity, he bought his mistresses and his wife a big volume of cheap shoes from justfab.com. He wiped off traces of calls and text messages to his women; he took Jersey Shore for dinner only on weekdays. I was aware of all these facts because Jersey Shore was Terrence and I's friend. I made a huge mistake by bailing her out from jail once. She never learned any lessons. Jersey Shore turned out to be desperately in love with Foreigner Boner, and she prioritized her relationships with married men and her own boss over her adorable daughter. The worst thing of all was Foreigner Boner lent his mistresses, who were mostly single moms, money at 12 percent interest rate. He thought he did a huge favor by lending them money at a lower interest rate.

We all think that Miami is a beautiful place with good folks, but a more accurate picture of Miami is people with no manners and flaky and shady people. Some deliberately do not speak English, and they are famous for their road rage. Hopefully it will change for the better with Generation Y. It is time to take Miami to the next level.

For a week, Terrence wrote me a heartbreaking letter and expressed his love for me. No matter what he said, promised, and talked about, nothing changed my mind. Terrence was cherishing hopes to get me back. The same weekend my niece arrived at Miami, he had arranged a BBQ in the park to impress my family. My niece did not like him right away. No one liked him. It was a beautiful day in the middle of March. Terrence and I had invited our friends as well. The entire time we were there, Terrence was getting jealous and antsy. I had already made my decision to break up with him, so I did not care.

"Dating in Miami is hard!" says Mike, Terrence's friend. "For my girlfriend, there is always a need to go out to a fancy restaurant to post her selfies on social media and make all our friends jealous."

Wanting to keep the conversation lively, I interjected, "Some women are chasing after something that is not wanted but needed. Some men and women are shallow, and they get jealous of friends' successful lives and hot and rich boyfriends and girlfriends. These women compare their lives to people they do not know of. Instead, they get deluded with the idea of chic and celebrities' lives from dumb reality shows. Some get afflicted with Kardashian-manic disease that makes all their men sick, lose their identity, and get depressed. These Kardashians have become famous out of dirt and sex tapes. Even their own dad turned into a woman called Caitlyn. It reminds me of a single-ladies group staying at the hotel just because the Kardashians stayed there. The dumb group asked me to even show them the suite the Kardashians stayed at. The more brainless the show is, the more popular they get. It shows how many idiotic and stupid people are out there."

I added, "A woman is different and unique in her way. A woman should have her money, stay feminine, be proud of accomplishments, make her man feel proud, contribute, and sometimes treat her man to a nice dinner or surprise him. Confident, independent, and intelligent women are way more attractive than naked hot bodies."

My conversation got interrupted by Terrence. The fact that he did not have a sense of tact annoyed the hell out of me. "Baby, can you please come here?" He was speaking to me in an imperative mood. His voice was unyielding and loud—dramatic. He was trembling, shaking, and shivering. He was trying hard. I pretended I could not hear him. "Come here!" he repeated in a very demanding tone of voice. He had been cooking the meat and BBQ all day.

"Why don't you let your friends cook the rest of the BBQ meat?"

"Why? You don't like the BBQ I cooked? I was here since nine a.m. I secured the place and have been cooking for all of you!" he yelled at the top of his lungs.

"Well, that is what you wanted, right? You wanted to make a good impression on my family."

Terrence was chewing a pork loin, and he took it out of his mouth, spat out the biggest piece, and chewed up the biggest pork on the floor in front of everyone. It was outrageous and embarrassing. Rum and coke neutralized my level of anger.

"I am out of here. F——y'all!" he yelled and started to grab all the food and his stuff.

"Get lost. This is the last time you'll see me." I laughed at him.

Everyone was in shock and frozen for a moment.

"No worries. He gets that way. Terrence stamps around the office like a child when he is pissed," said Mike.

I was so glad he behaved in an ugly way. It came in handy.

We bumped into each other on the street where he made a scene by getting down on his knee and asking me to give him one more chance. He was so intense and dramatic and thunderous. I hate loud, moody, and emotional people for the fact that immature and rude behavior makes other people feel uncomfortable.

"What's love got to do with it? You are very immature. You are jumping from one place to the other. Your daughter dislikes you. You have chosen me over your child. If I were in your ex's shoes, I would have filed for child support on your ass long time ago. I do not love you. I never loved you. I was just curious why some women can't go back once they go black. My curiosity got satisfied."

"You hurt me deeply, and my heart is bleeding."

"I do not give a damn about your heart."

I walked away from him and never looked back. I went back to finding a mature, smart, and good-hearted man.

What not to date:

- Men who are irresponsible
- Men who abandon their children
- Men who do not contribute even if he stays at your place all the time
- Men who know they are great lovers but consider that great sex entitles them to free housing
- Men who are immature
- Men who make bad decisions all the time
- Men who have bad genetics and terrible family upbringing
- Men whose coworkers do not respect him or consider him rude and incompetent

CHAPTER 7

Leverage

I WAS BACK ON TINDER and was shuffling through profiles. I was looking at few profile pictures that were set in the mosaic format. If you'd zoom in and take a closer look, some of them were ugly. Do not trust the images of half-naked guys lying in bed. It is clear and obvious: these guys are into themselves. The chances that they are introverted or they have some health or mental issues or erectile dysfunction are high. Here's one interesting fact I discovered about the importance of asymmetry in your facial features: if you have one eye smaller than the other, a slightly different angle of the right eyebrow makes it breathtaking. If you use a photo robot and add the most beautiful eyes, nose, eyebrows, great cheekbones, and perfect full lips, the face turns into the freakiest and ugliest face.

I came across the profile of the most handsome man ever. It was a great night; I met the hottest guy online. Richard with the angle of his dangle wanted me back; immature Terrence was dying to get me back. I think once you get someone, all your exes feel it and they want you back. Terrence sent me pictures of him all dressed up and lying down on top of a Mustang. If only these two could see the new hottest boyfriend I had ever had.

I was getting so excited and nervous at the same time; I needed a drink right then. What made me nervous was I had never dated a model. My perception of models is they are selfish and can be intimidating. I know that I am pretty, but I am not gorgeous. I thought, *Well, I will just have fun and not think about where it is going.* His name was Jeffrey. He looked like an actor, Matt Bomer from the *White Collar* series. In his picture, Jeffrey had green eyes and was six three tall. He had dark-brown hair, unbuttoned shirt showing off his body, strong jawline, and big veiny hands. His father was Italian, and his mom was Native American. For safety reasons, we agreed to meet at a lounge in Midtown Miami.

I was already feeling tipsy good. I needed to get drunk-brave before he got there. Here he came. My face exploded into the biggest smile. He was exactly how he looked in his picture. He was very well-dressed in white, a fitted Armani shirt and stylish jeans. He lingered toward me and kissed me on a cheek. Jeff was holding my hand; our hands fit perfectly. He had big hands that wrapped my small hands. Jeff called my hands little bird hands. He showed up with his buddy who was goofy, obnoxious, and average-looking. The chemistry was instant. Everything looked good on paper. Jeff had the looks and personality. He drove an expensive car. He had fashion sense, preferred fine dining, and carried an engaging conversation.

"I like you, Alexandra. I like you so much, you are like home to me."

"I like you too." It melted my heart.

Instantly, we indulged in a passionate kiss. Butterflies were flying all over my tummy as it got intense and arousing. *I should not sleep with Jeff tonight, but he is in town only until tomorrow. I am not sure if I will see him ever again.* The night was magical; we made love seven times. Jeffrey made love passionately and did it with finesse. What is it with Italian men? I am certain there must be something in Italian pasta and sausage.

I presumed beforehand that models were shallow and brainless. To my biggest surprise, Jeffrey turned out to be knowledgeable about comprehensive history and corporate America, and he had a great personality. In his eyes, I was the sexiest woman he'd ever met in his life.

He drove back to Tampa the very next morning. I was beyond excited and ecstatic. Our phone conversations were deep and meaningful. For me, a man who intellectually challenges me is the most handsome and sexiest man on earth. He was beautiful inside out. It is such a rarity to find an all-in-one person these days. Weeks of interesting conversations turned into conversations about his wealthy friends, inheritance, and evil family. According to Jeffrey, he had inherited millions from his grandfather, but he had no access to his money yet. There was a huge family feud. Jeffrey was against greedy and mean and evil relatives who wanted to keep all the money and leave him out of the trust fund. He had a very rough childhood. His dad's health was deteriorating, and vicious relatives were careless about his dad. Even though his father had chosen his mistresses over his only son, Jeffrey was taking care of his sick dad.

"You are the only good thing in life. I appreciate you and am so thankful for everything you do for me," said Jeff.

All he was telling me touched me deeply. I think when we are into someone, every little thing or word or compliment makes our day.

"Soon we'll be together, and everything will be better and greater," promised Jeffrey.

Our friendship was getting stronger. If you are my good friend, I'll do my best to help you. If I like a guy, I buy him a gift and try to help him if needed. On one of his bad days, he did not have any money for food. I ran to the post office and sent him Korean and Japanese snacks and money through Western Union. I even made traditional kimchi and sent it to him. I had not done that for anybody. I must had been in love with him. Love was in the air.

"I will try to do my best to make it to Miami this weekend. Can you please check out a couple lofts in the Wynwood area?"

"Of course, I will be glad to help you. You will be my neighbor."

I was already imagining him moving into a big and nicely decorated loft. I would be cooking dinner, and we would be drinking a good wine together and having amazing sex every night.

Labor Day weekend approached. Jeffrey was making plans to see me. But for the second time, he could not make it. I started feeling that something was off. For men, out of sight means out of mind.

"Hi, baby, what are you doing? Can you go and find out if the Apple store in Miami Beach has the Apple Watch that is coming out tomorrow?" asked Jeffrey.

"Of course, you can preorder today and get it tomorrow. Doesn't Orlando have Apple stores?" I got curious.

"They do, but they are an hour and a half drive from my house. I want that Apple Watch so badly." His voice sounded desperate.

"I want you, Jeff." I tried to switch the subject, as I was getting irritated.

"If you want me, then go and get me an Apple Watch!" Jeff snickered.

Hot water splashed my face. "I have to let you go, Jeffrey. I believe you are looking for someone to maintain you and take care of you." I hung up on him.

The very next morning, Jeffrey used his articulate skills and made me understand that I overreacted and took his jokes the wrong way.

"Do you know I was very successful?" boasting Jeffrey said. He was bragging about his successful modeling career with Versace, Tom Ford, and Armani. He was dwelling on his past often lately, which I found as a sign that he was asking for compliments. I was not used to complimenting a man on his beauty. I got the compliments.

"The past has already passed. It is all about what you do about it now," I said in a slightly irritated voice.

Jeffrey always knew how to change the subject when he did not like my straightforwardness. He did not like my honest opinion about people who constantly blame the past and their family and lack of luck. What I meant to say was this: "Deal with it, grow up, and shut the hell up. Do something about it. Make a change." Instead I asked him questions to dumb down to his level. "Have you dated a model?" I asked him.

"No, and I never will."

"Why?" I was curious.

"They are mean and vicious."

"They do not eat at all. I can't imagine how cranky I'd get if I do not eat sumptuous food. The models don't have any options. They eat cotton balls instead of food," I carried the conversation.

I thought if I were a gorgeous top model and had a hot body, I would be angry all the time. I love food so much. My palate must be satisfied. Food, company, and great sex are the main three pleasures of mine. I want to try new dishes and be open to all foods and cultures.

Finally, Jeffrey settled on a plan: he wanted to rent a loft near me, get a modeling job during the day, bartend at a gay club at night, and have me move in with him once my lease was up. Brilliant plan! Christmas was around the corner. Love was still in the air.

"It would be great if you come over to Orlando for Christmas," Jeff begged me.

"How bad do you want me?" I slightly flirted.

"Baby, please. I need you now more than ever. My dad was diagnosed with kidney cancer."

"I will be there, and I'll help you with your dad."

I felt bad and sad about his father and was feeling but-terflies again. I booked my flight and did not eat dinner for a week. I shredded five pounds. I was feeling good. I needed to lose fifteen pounds to look my best.

"You look great," he complimented me.

I was wearing a tight leather skirt with a baby-pink see-through blouse. Honestly, he looked like a Russian saying: "His face was run down by a truck." He had dry skin, which always makes anyone look older and unhealthy.

"You look good too," I complimented, knowing all men love compliments—especially models die for compliments.

"No, I don't. I need to take better care of my skin," said Jeff.

The first day I arrived, I wanted to visit his sick dad in the hospital, but Jeffrey told me his dad hated Koreans and Vietnamese. I am Korean; most of us are friendly and hardworking people. Apparently, his grandfather was in the Vietnam War, and he told his entire family and friends about how bad Vietnamese people were. Well, it was a war. Soldiers kill and torture enemies.

I checked into a hotel located two miles from his parents' house. Jeffrey started to undress me without any emotions. His face looked like he was unbuttoning his shirt after he came from work and was looking in the bathroom mirror. His big boy grew up to 8.3 inches and turned thick, beautiful, and wanted.

"I know you love my big boy. He loves you," unemotional Jeff said and pushed me down.

He loved blow jobs in the mornings, nights, and sponta-neously throughout the day. I got aroused, but I felt awkward. The moment he slid into my wetness, I heard him saying, "I need financial help. I need to pay for my phone."

I pretended not to pay attention and asked him to love and fuck me. His veiny neck, green eyes, and six-pack turned me on.

I glanced at his veiny arms and wrist and saw the Apple Watch on his wrist. *Wait a minute. It is the Apple Watch.* And it just hit me. He had someone else who supported him financially and bought him the wanted Apple Watch. We had a quickie.

"Do it faster and deeper and harder," I whispered in his ears.

The night was empty and lonely.

The next morning, we stopped by a grocery store, and he asked me to stay with his dogs in the car. I waited for long twenty minutes and got out of the car and took a walk with dogs. And all of a sudden, I heard him yelling at me, "Why did you get out of the car? I told you to stay in the car. All these people keep staring at the dogs." Jeff looked pissed.

"I do not like the tone of your voice. And what is wrong with people staring at your dogs? They're just dogs."

I realized something. Jeffrey's ex-girlfriend bought him a car under her name. I recalled him mentioning it. Jeffrey was afraid that his and his ex's friends in common would see him and his new girlfriend.

"Sorry. I was mean to you," Jeff apologized when we got back to the hotel room.

"I understand you are under a lot of pressure, but I am going to change my ticket to a day earlier. I am not happy here with you. I came here to support you. You could have been nicer to me. I am going to fly out tomorrow morning."

"Go ahead, and you, too, run away," Rage Flare said.

"Your negativity brings me down all the time. I don't think I want to be with someone who brings me down." I sighed disappointedly.

I returned home and was feeling used. Jeff was using all these women who believed him and felt sorry about his sick dad. I remember him saying that the trust fund would make him very rich soon and he would pay all the money back to me.

Our long-distance relationship lasted five months. The level of excitement went down, and the conversations dumbed down significantly. Jeff used emojis for everything. I considered it a degrading act. If he couldn't articulate emotions or he had nothing to say, then he had bunch of hay instead of brains. Now I think about how fast he sent me his dick pics, pictures of him in the shower and in the forest half-naked on a horse, and fashion show pics—in a heartbeat. Every morning, he used to send me his dick pick, the same images. He most likely texted all his pics in the order that was received by all women. The sequence of all images was the same for five months.

I am quite sure he used his camouflage. Under his impressive looks, he was good for nothing. His strategy was to impress a woman with his knowledge about worldwide history, politics, corporate America; his profound sense of humor; and the promise of his soon-to-be-rich status. He used the same script: he lost his job, his dad got sick with cancer, his stepmom was mean to him, his entire family hated him and they were kicking him out, etc.

This was my last email to Loser-User:

Hi Jeff:

Hope this Email finds you well. I feel you played with my feelings. I flew up to see you, but you made me feel terrible. You played me for a fool. The worst you've done is made me believe your lies. It was a waste of my valuable time and another disappointment for me.

I am not mad at you but myself. You did not have enough balls to be honest with me, or you simply don't respect me. You are a cruel person, Jeffrey, and turned out to be a

big asshole. I do not need any more bullshit.
I want you to know I had trust issues and
opened my heart to you only, and you completely ruined it. You came up with so many
lies to use women. You are Loser-User. You
should know that you are very self-centered.
You were always talking about you, your past
all the time. But life is present, now and it is
not about what you have done in the past but
what you are doing about it now. I leave it at
that. Take care. And go and kiss my big and
round Asian ass.

This was his response to me:

>You have no room to talk.
>I was cool w/you & your last conversa-
>tion w/me secured my opinion that I don't
>know you fully.
>Hence, me trying to reason w/you over
>n over.
>Your responses were negative and I quote
>"BLAH BLAH BLAH."
>I'm sorry, but who the fuck do you think
>you are?
>I was trying to have an adult conversa-
>tion w/you. I don't need your disrespectful
>attitude!!!
>I just needed your understanding. You
>talked plenty of yourself, too! That's fine I
>wanted to know.
>I'm appreciative of things you've done
>for me as well.

No one was played here.

I'm trying to get myself together that's all.

There is a side of you that I don't like at all and won't tolerate it.

It's the "BLAH BLAH BITCH" side.

Again, it's not about me not caring because I do.

Kiss your round ass? I've done that.

I'm not going to cut you down or this n that.

I just don't need that right now.

Sorry you feel this way.

His email made my blood boil. I sent him a pic of my ex who looked like Bradley Cooper and wrote this on top of the picture: "Meet my new boyfriend. He is a successful doctor. And better lover than you are. You need to relax and be less angry and hateful about everything and everyone in your life."

"You are such a bitch," he responded.

"I would rather be a bitch than someone you use to get money. I feel pity for you. You dwell on the past. I hope you find a piece of your mind and heart. Get a job and do something you love to do. Stop using vulnerable and strong women. Please find a sugar mama, and you will be happy! You get paid, your sugar mama is satisfied—a perfect arrangement."

Jeff's sperm needed some anger management, and they were looking for a sugar mama. Each sperm looked like matches with angry red faces on the tips. They were embittered and antagonistic. I called his sperms Rage Flare. Rage Flare did not drink and couldn't take the edge off. They talked like the comedian Lewis Black, they angry-ranted through hour-long conversations, they stood still, idle, and always worked out in a home-based gym. Rage Flare always looked for sugar mamas. Hot and strongly hung young men. Rage Flare's ass would get tighter, and they couldn't relax the muscles. They'd meet sugar mamas and get derailed out of their way, but they still couldn't relax their asshole's muscles.

That same weekend, I decided to have a full spa weekend and clear my head. Vietnamese nail technicians always gossip and talk shit about all their clients in their language. I consider the Vietnamese language very unpleasant to the ears, and the skillful gossiping in front of their customers are signs of stupidity.

"Do you have a boyfriend?" Nosy one asked me.

"No. It is not easy to find a good man these days."

I briefly told her about Jeffrey to feed her hunger to blabbing. Her eyes lit up, and she kept gossiping: "One of my friends is a very wealthy lady. She met this young and gorgeous man. Now she sends him money. She bought him an iPhone and Apple Watch and even bought him a car. She owns the candy factory up in northeast. And her boy toy lives in Miami." The useless chat was enthusiastic to tell me all the details as if I were interested.

One year later, the liar, loser, and user contacted me via Facebook Messenger right before Christmas. He moved to Miami because his stepmom kicked him out. His ex-girlfriend apparently took her car back. She was making all the car payments. Jeff was still hoping to get an access to his trust fund.

How do assholes like him get away with using and taking advantage of women? How do they convince us, and what makes us trust these narcissistic, full of shit, angry, and lazy trust fund babies?

In the mind of Loser-User Jeff and anus of Rage Flare, his gorgeous looks and huge penis leveraged his traditional obligations as a man, breadwinner, and friend.

All his blah blah blah : "Do you remember us, my big boy, and everything that we had?" "You are not the sweet person I once knew," "I thought that you cared about me," "You cannot even meet me after everything we have done," "You do not care that I have no place to go tonight, I have no money for food, my mom kicked me out, and I am homeless."

I bet all the women he used in the past got fed up with Loser-User. He was screening his phone and texting all women with bait. His bait to catch someone's attention was his images and dick pics gallery. Once again, preconceived notions of attractiveness made me choose the wrong guy. Well, I had him figured out within five months.

What not to date:

- Former broke-ass model
- He says he inherited millions, but he has no access to his millions yet
- He always sends you his pictures—naked pictures and dick pics
- He always talks about how mean his family is
- He always talks bad about his ex and is always angry at everybody
- He always worries about his looks and never smiles
- He details his upbringing by five women his dad dated

CHAPTER 8

Athletic Sperm—Guaranteed

Two years after I broke off my engagement, dated bunch of losers, and met disappointment after disappointment, I was single again. Urgently, I needed to go out. I was with my coworkers in Redbar drinking cocktails and dancing. It was September 11, 2010. My friend Ella was a professional dancer. Whenever we went out, we always had fun. I was younger, and I was tipsy that night at the Redbar in Brickell. Ella came back from the restroom with two good-looking guys. "Alexandra, meet Chris and Alejandro."

"Great to meet you guys." I kept dancing.

"Your guy is hot, and he is a future doctor!"

"This is my favorite song. Let us dance." I was so into dancing, and I did not even care about a future doctor. *I wonder if he can dance. White boys can't dance,* I assumed.

I looked at his big juicy lips. Typically, white Caucasian men have thin lips, which I find very unattractive. Thin lips look like a striking line, and you can't suck thin lines with no puffy fat and juice on them. *He better be a good kisser.*

They say white boys can't dance. But Chris was half-Latin. He got moves like Channing Tatum. I wondered if it was true that if you can't dance or swim, you suck in bed. Looking at how Chris danced, he must had been a great sex machine.

"We are going to another club. Do you want to come with us?" asked Chris.

"Does it have good music and good cocktails?" I asked very enthusiastically.

He pulled me and started kissing me and said in a very masculine voice, "Anything you want."

I almost drowned in his mouth; the way he was kissing was like a big wave hitting my lips.

"You are sexy, Alexandra. You are like an Asian porn star. Come here, my Asian Persuasion," said Chris.

It turned me on. We ended up having sex that night until seven the next morning. We both were enjoying each other's company so much and were into each other. After ten times of intense and amazing sex, we were sexed out and passed out. Our chemistry was so intense and incredible all night long.

Anastasia commented this on our picture: "Alexandra, you have to do everything possible to marry this guy. You are a perfect couple. He is an anesthesiologist; your father is a doctor. You look good together. You look so happy, Alexandra."

A year later, Chris moved to the Dominican Republic to get his anesthesiology degree. Since 2011, we had been seeing each other on and off for four years. In all honesty, I was not a saint, and I was seeing other guys too. Undoubtedly, Chris was seeing other girls. We all have our needs. My needs must be satisfied as well as his.

I used to pick him up in my convertible with Vivaldi's *The Four Seasons* playing loudly during his lunch breaks when he was in town. No wonder they say that doctors are the horniest and biggest womanizers among professionals. It is much easier to get quickies. They know anatomy and biology inside out, so they have a deeper knowledge of all the body's reactions and responses. One of the common characteristics that always attracted me was doctors' profound sense of humor.

Chris always had stories about his patients. There was a patient with a tennis ball in his ass. The patient had a poker face, and he kept denying the fact that he or his gay partner put a tennis ball inside his ass. We both laughed so hard that we could feel it in our lungs, so hard that it took our breath away.

Another funny emergency case was when doctors in the emergency room found a remote control in a patient's ass. The doctors were joking, saying, "When he farts, it changes the channel. Depending on how long and chaotic he farts, more likely, the gay porn movie on demand would turn on unmistakably."

Chris's knowledge about history, politics, people, loyalty, friendship, family values, strongest people, relationship complications, manhood, and femininity always impressed me and made me crave for more interesting, intellectually stimulating, and deeper conversations. We both enjoyed soulful and intelligent conversations and appreciated the luxury of having a companion and partner you could talk about anything. We discussed the importance of upbringing, always improving, and working toward your goals. And the fact that we both loved classical music by Antonio Vivaldi, Wolfgang Mozart, Sebastian Bach, and Samuel Barber made me realize how much I was falling for Chris every time I saw him. We used to spoon and listen to our favorite collection of classical music. It was our music, us being happy and electrified and satisfied sexually.

Chris was a great basketball and golf player. I loved that about him. Most of the men I had dated were not into sports, which I found unattractive. I remember when he would take me to watch him play basketball games. It always turned me on. I felt I was the best cheerleader wearing my shirt and denim shorts and pigtails and cheering so loud that all the other girls hated me. Seeing Chris running and scoring the highest for his team, all sweaty, made me all wet. After the game, the night was something indescribable. The way he made love to me and kissed me from head to toe while hearing him say, "Baby, you make me so happy. I want you, all of you" made me feel incredible in a way I had never felt before.

In November 2013, I got a call at work. The receptionist called my extension and said there was a guy named Chris waiting for me in the lobby. My heart was beating like the heart of a blue-throated hummingbird.

"I was looking for you all over. I lost my phone. I called Hilton Hotels in Miami and asked for a Korean Russian. A lot of people know you. I am proud of you! I want to take you out for dinner."

"A guy who was looking for me deserves to take me out." I giggled.

After deep conversations and a sumptuous dinner that night, we were into each other so deep, we did it ten times. His unexplainable passionate chemistry was filling us up every time we saw each other.

"I have to go back to the Dominican Republic for a year and a half to finish my school. When I get back, we'll be together. I care about you deeply," he promised me.

Was he the one? We had everything. We had sex and communication, both of us came from very good families, and we were both very ambitious, healthy, driven, and very much career-oriented. And I feel I could trust him. What else could a woman want? We would be fundamentally happy people. I was so high at this moment.

In 2015, Chris came back to Miami for good. He had finished school. I was so proud of him. He finally did it!

"I missed you so bad," said Chris as he hugged me tightly.

"I was confident in you. Congrats. Very proud of you." My eyes were twinkling.

"I want to invite you to dinner," Chris said with a little of nervousness in his voice.

After a few cocktails and delicious sushi, we ended up in a hotel room on South Beach. Endless lovemaking and incredible chemistry remained the same five years later.

"I have to tell you something. I have a daughter. I did not know about her existence until last month. I had to do a paternity test because the mother of my daughter got pregnant and left school. She has trapped me, told me she was on birth control."

I fell off the bed. I had to contain myself. My heart fell to my ankles.

"Congrats! You've become a father. Why are you telling me after you made love to me? Why? To hurt me?" I sprinted out of bed and rushed to get dressed and get the hell out of the room. "You are the biggest piece of shit, liar, and coward. How can you be so smart and stupid at the same time?" I was holding my tears. Chris was not going to see me cry.

"Please do not go. I love you. I want to be with you. I wanted to get divorced, but my wife is pregnant with the second child."

"What? You are worthless!" I yelled and flew out of the room.

I knew he would be calling me, so I blocked his number. I was so hurt and in pain. I was letting him go this time. I just couldn't comprehend and understand him. Later, I researched, and I found out all these facts via social media: He was engaged in 2012; he got married in 2013. All this time, he had been lying to me and telling me that he still wanted me and cared about me a lot. The worst was that he lied about not knowing about the existence of his daughter. He said, "She is a bitch. All she wants is my money. She trapped me with this pregnancy. She is manipulating me through our children and blah, blah, blah."

Honestly speaking, I was not a saint. I was dating other guys while he was out of the country and getting his anesthesiology degree. I couldn't be angry at him because we were not in a committed relationship. It was my fault, as I had expectations and I filled my head with all the bullcrap and did not want to accept the truth. If a man does not commit to you for years, he's just using you for sex and pleasure.

I had to say goodbye to long-awaited Chris and his athletic sperm.

I think we should use single stallion assholes for sex with no strings attached and value good guys more. What I should do from now on is withhold sex with good guys for three months and make a good guy fall in love with me first.

Sometimes we are hard on ourselves, and we regret that we were not aggressive enough or that we did not pursue that great guy. Let the man pursue me. I am not chasing after anyone anymore. Times have changed. These days, women do not need men. Women need warriors. I felt incredibly stronger and more powerful. As Honoré de Balzac puts it, "Power does not consist in striking with force or with frequency, but in striking true."

Success is the best revenge. I will build my hotel empire and be happy with a great man. I will be sailing on my boat and sipping champagne and oysters with the love of my life.

What not to date:

- Separated, almost divorced men
- Liars
- Cheaters
- Fanatic religious men
- Men who come up with stories about abusive ex-wives and entrapment with pregnancy twice or who give the excuse that she said she was on birth control
- Cowards
- Guys who disappear for months and appear when they are miserable
- Guys who break your heart

CHAPTER 9

Skinny Bitches, He Is All Yours!

I LOVED MY LIFE! I lived in paradise; I was healthy and full of life. I lost weight, and I was feeling good about my body. They say you'll meet someone who will love you for exactly who you are—with muffin top or without, love handles, untoned arms, imperfect skin. It would not matter. If you like someone, you accept them with all their flaws.

Great weather calls for mimosas and pool. The pools in my building were humongous, and the views of Biscayne Bay and the downtown skyline were fantastic. I brought champagne and orange juice with me. While taking a dip in our heated pool, I heard a man's voice with a German accent. I always like German guys because Germans are known for invention, being meticulous, and their resourcefulness.

Both of us drank two bottles of champagne and got so tipsy a few hours later. We ended up at his loft. His mom helped him decorate his loft; it was white, black, and purple, which I found unique. His company imported flowers from Central America.

Matthias was good-looking, but he was kind of into himself and was an excessive germophobe. Every time I touched the table or put my arms on the table, he would grab a paper towel and wipe Windex on it. He would be flexing his arms in front of me and constantly looking in the mirror and checking himself out all the time. His German sausage was long but not thick enough. I was puzzled. What would be better and more pleasurable? Long and thin or short and thick? Hard floor or bouncy mattress? What about shape or angle? To me, it just had to be a perfect size, be thick, and have a perfect angle.

I stayed at his place a few times. It was always predictable. I would cook good Uzbek food. He would take me out for dinner. He was always bragging about how great Germany was and that they made the best cars in the world. He was so competitive when I would bring up Italians and continue to bet, argue, and dispute over who made the best cars. Germans are very direct and punctual, and they love soccer and their beer.

It made Matthias look charming when he would bring me flowers. Sex with Matthias was all right. The weekend was approaching. Matthias took me for Sunday brunch at a Greek restaurant in Brickell. Mimosas were pouring in with a delicious brunch and interesting conversation about life, personalities, and international relations between the USA and Europe.

"What interests you the most in women?"

"Great personality and intelligence. I love Asian women, but they must be skinny. If you lose weight, Alexandra, you would be hot. Let me show you my Filipina girlfriend."

My eyes reflected resentment, and Matthias's eyes showed he realized he said something stupid. Men must choose words carefully. I imagined his sperm as skinny entities speaking to one another about how skinny was sexy. I looked at the picture and saw the skinniest girl. She looked unhealthy, like skin wrapped around bones.

"So what are you going to do if you get married to a skinny girl and she gets pregnant and gains weight? Naturally, women gain weight while they are pregnant."

"I will put her on a diet and lock her in a closet with water and crackers. My mom looks great in her fifties. I want my wife to look hot."

"Why is everybody complaining about their looks but not their brains?" I took an act of revenge on him.

"We are men, very visual. We get attracted to what we find beautiful, and the women do not have to be all that smart. If they look good, feed me, fuck good, and let me watch soccer, that is all I want."

I was in shock the moment I heard it. He was just a regular guy with pathetic shallowness.

"I receive good and sexy compliments," I said in a hissy fit.

"Come on. You are a confident woman. I was pretty sure that it would not affect your level of confidence because you are a cute, very strong, and confident woman."

"I wish you the best of luck with your skinny to-be wife. Looks are all temporary—no matter what surgery or how ageist you are. Just accept aging with grace and pride. Extra fat or calories on your body should not be shameful, but the lack of common sense and intellect is a shame."

"Do not get philosophical on me, Alexandra. That stuff does not turn me on. I don't care about how smart the women are. Do you want to have dinner with me?"

That same weekend, Matthias invited me to dinner at the top steak house in Miami with the most expensive wine. My plan to embarrass him could not have come at a better time for revenge. I inhaled a juicy steak, drank my wine fast, and ordered a dessert without overthinking. When it comes to menu ordering, I get very decisive. Matthias excused himself to use the bathroom. While he was in the restroom, I squeezed some eye drops in his cocktail. It made him run to the bathroom and shit in his pants the next day. I will be laughing at him for as long as I live, and he will be embarrassed and will remember me forever. Bye, bye, bye, German Shallow Ass.

A year later, I bumped into him and his thin but unpleasant girlfriend with an ugly face. He looked the same, and his eyes were still gazing at other skinny women. Some men never change. Nothing changes.

What not to date:

- Jerks who tell you to lose weight
- Guys who are into skinny girls only, no exception
- Germophobes
- Shallow men

CHAPTER 10

Baby Mama Drama

MIAMI IS AN IMAGE-CONSCIOUS CITY, where it is all about boobs and ass. Well, 80 percent of the female population has done plastic surgeries from head to toe. If you want to be marketable in the dating arena, you must be very fit and sexy. To fit in and feel good about myself, I joined a local gym. It was a very cool concept and was full of good-looking guys. The gyms can be intimidating to some people, but for me, they are very motivating. If you look good, you feel good!

I was doing squats, and a cute Latin guy asked me, "Do you want to work out together?"

"Why not? What do I have to do?"

"Can you pass me that ball?" David asked me.

I giggled and asked him, "Which ball—red or blue?"

He burst out laughing. "I want you to pass me the red ball."

After the blue-and-red-ball-passing session, I gave him my phone number. He waited three days to call me. I guess he followed the famous three-day rule. David was a firefighter. He was kind and the father of two beautiful daughters. *How would he be in bed?* I wondered. I had never dated or had sex with Latin guys. My friends had told me that Latin men make great lovers.

We were at a Brazilian steak house in Midtown drinking Malbec and enjoying our conversation. With a craving for a juicy steak and very frothy dessert, I was salivating as I looked at the menu. We were laughing and talking about the education system in the USA. He was teaching emergency care. How adorable!

"I love teachers and professors. I wanted to be a math teacher," I said to David.

"You would be a sexy teacher, and I would be your bad student so that you can give me extra tutoring in math at nights." I got David excited.

"You have a great imagination, Alexandra."

"You have no idea. But there is only one way to live the fantasy with me."

"It sounds intriguing and provocative."

"Impress me." He gave me the I-want-you look. I decided to build it up by not having sex right away.

"How about we are to be at the bar tomorrow night and pretend not to know each other?"

It was 8:00 p.m., and with butterflies in my stomach and a sense of intense arousal, I entered a small and very intimate bar on South Beach. There were only twenty-five seats. I loved this new concept. The closer we got, the more excited we got about lingering as we occasionally touched or rubbed each other's hands.

I was in a black lace dress with an open back. I had screaming red lips and less eye makeup. *My flawless skin, red lips that pop, and captivating looks will get me a great lover tonight.* I sat two seats away from him. He wore a Zara shirt, and I could see the sexiest buttocks. Did I forget to mention that he had a knockout body?

"Hi, how are you doing tonight?" He was staring at me.

"Outstanding." I smiled at him.

"I am Jack. What brings you to Miami?"

"Vacation."

"How is it going?"

"Looking at you, it is going very well," I flirted.

"I must say, you are beautiful, and you have a nice smile."

"Thank you. You, too, are good-looking."

He got me lychee martinis and vodka and tonic. We kissed so much that my lips got very puffy, and my cheeks got pink naturally. I loved kissing him.

Then we heard someone behind us say, "David." His ex-wife sounded so loud, and she was walking into the restaurant. She gave me a look with a fake smile. She was with her man. No offense, my lovely friends, but I consider that Latin women can be dramatic. You have no idea how miraculously ex-wives appear at places. She reminded me of my ex-roommate, a decade older than me. She was an Argentinean chick who dragged me and begged me to run to all the places where the father of her kids was. She was a very skillful stalker. Her name was Carolina. She would say with her dramatic and Argentinean accent, "It is meant to be, *mi amor*." Her obsession would make him roll his eyes and want to get in and out, as he used her for quickies during his lunch breaks or right before he went out with his boys. I have heard that some artists like to have sex before going on the stage to look mysterious, sexier, and more desirable. He was a very good-looking Argentinean German, but he was a jerk. I called him Peacock. She appreciated his honesty and still wanted him even after the fact that Argentinean German Peacock infected her with herpes. A few years later, he became VP of business development at a high-tech company and got married, but not to her. It was evident that he would never marry a girl with no sense of humor and who was unintelligent and desperate. I recall myself guffawing at the comedy show she dragged me to, to stalk Argentinean

German Peacock. She did not get the humor about racial jokes. I think racial jokes are funny as well as jokes about fanatic religious people. In general, individuals who can laugh at themselves are happier and more intelligent in life.

I disliked her for another reason: she was stuck-up and always made bad comments about Korean food—"I hate your stinky kimchi" "How can you eat beef?" She was vegan. I am sure she was faking it to make an impression on guys. I consider some insane and passionate dog lovers as fake, lonely, and weak people—especially the ones who own little Chihuahuas. These loud minidogs are purposeless. They bark annoyingly loud, and they do not serve a purpose. If you want to have a dog, get a Siberian husky or French bulldog or boxer.

One weekend of many, I had a bad hangover. When we nonvegans have a hangover, we order greasy food such as pizzas, burgers, tacos, or Denny's. She saw me eating a juicy burger with mushrooms and caramelized onions and moaning as the burger was so juicy, yummy, and fatty.

"That looks disgusting. What you are eating, Alexandra?" She made a face with her duck lips. "Do you know how they slaughter cows?"

"I do not care, Carolina. I am starving now, and if it looks good, I eat it."

That skinny bitch was always making fun of my plump figure. It fired me up, and I told her off after I had finished my juicy burger and said to her, laughing at her skinny ass, "Did you know that in Korea, well-bred dogs' meat was a delicacy many years ago? You need to take better care of your dogs. They are shitting everywhere because you don't walk them for days. If you ever make a disrespectful comment about my food one more time, your dogs will disappear."

I scared her. Like Russians say, "If people are afraid of you, they respect you." That was what I wanted. Mission accomplished. One should be respectful of another's culture and food. And I told her not mess with Koreans about their food. The look on her face was priceless. I wish I could take a picture of her duck lips and scared face. I noticed that people with facial plastic surgeries have the ugliest and most unattractive facial expressions and smiles.

I was wondering at that moment why some Argentineans are condescending and stuck-up. They think they are elite and crème de la crème of South America. I say it is a bullcrap. We all are aware of the fact that most Argentineans of European descent moved to South America between 1857 and 1940. Among them were Italians, Germans, and Jews. They fled their countries and got accepted in most South American countries; mainly Jews immigrated the most during and after World War II. I find their arrogance as the main reason why all Miamians can't stand Argentineans. From my experience, Italians from Italy are nicer than Argentinean Italians, Germans from Germany are very cool, Argentinean Germans are even more arrogant, and Argentinean Jews are sneaky and stingy. German Jewish men are very cocky, which I find ironic and a double curse.

A few days later, I was looking for a place, as I found out that our place was up for foreclosure. Carolina kicked out her boyfriend who bought the place and took me as a roommate to use my rent for her vacations and savings. She was not as dumb as I thought.

Is it a coincidence or a common factor about some Argentinean women? I recall working with an Argentinean at one of the hotels in North Miami Beach. She was incompetent and obnoxious, and she used to come to work drunk and high. Her name was Sheila. She used my email to Ruthless Fraud to take revenge on me for firing her incompetent and lazy ass. Sheila forwarded my letter to the owners of the hotel I applied to. Sheila also badmouthed about few good hoteliers that eliminated their chances to get a job. She did me a big favor—the hotel my friends and I applied to was set to be sold and torn down. Then rumors circulated that the owners of those hotels were terrible people. They treated their employees terribly and simply did not care about the wellness of their employees, who'd make or break the hotel business.

David and I were seeing each other every other day. In the middle of one night, he woke up me up with a passionate kiss all over my body. The night we spent was of the best and with the most orgasms I had ever had. It was very hard to make me have a big O, but this Latin lover knew how to satisfy and devour me. I finally satisfied my sex fantasy with a hot Latin man. It was one of those nights. We got into the lotus Kama Sutra position. I wrapped my legs around him, and the moment he was thrusting in and out, Baby Mama Drama was calling him nonstop. She was crying over the phone, begging him to come to her house and saying that his daughters were crying and wanting to see their daddy. It just ruined the intense moment and made me dry. He had to leave and drive to his ex-wife's house. It turned out his ex-wife just wanted to see him and used the kids to dramatize and manipulate him. Perhaps her current boyfriend did not satisfy her. David returned home quickly with his hard-on and attacked me right at the door. We had done almost all the positions from the Kama Sutra: lotus, the Amazon, peg, star, rider, eagle, and much more. He could not get enough, and we did it ten times in one night.

"What a stellar and award-winning stamina you have, David!"

I wanted to keep spicing things up. I brought to life another fantasy of his to satisfy him more: I dressed up as a pizza delivery girl in a school-girl outfit with fishnet stockings, reading glasses, and the famous pigtails to complete the look. I picked up a pizza in that outfit. The building security officer's jaw dropped, and he did not even call David before he let me in and directed me to apartment 1507. I rang the door, and I did not see my Latin lover but an even hotter guy who looked like William Levy.

"Sorry, wrong apartment."

Wrong apartment's guy got creative. "I got all you need here, baby. Come on in."

"Did you order pizza?"

"I did just now. I am impressed how fast the delivery girl is!" said Wrong Guy.

We both laughed.

"Here is my card. Please come back anytime with the same outfit."

I rushed to David's apartment. The correct apartment number was 1607. David opened the door, and his jaw dropped. He blushed and said in his very macho tone, "I am not going to tip you. You are late, and you owe me a service recovery fee for delivering late."

"Anything. Please do not tell my boss, or I will lose my job."

He grabbed me and pushed me to the glass door and went down on me. Rain was drumming music, washing off the balcony windows. My naked body was steaming up the glass door, and David took me over from behind.

We were making love this time better than in *Fifty Shades of Grey* (that movie is overrated anyway). It was so good that he was screaming every time, and we felt euphoric. I slept tight that night; I was drooling.

A few days later, he invited me for homemade dinner. It was chicken-and-vegetables fried rice and salad. I brought Malbec wine, the type of wine we both like. I loved David's cooking. *What is the ingredient that makes the food incredibly sumptuous?*

"I like you Alexandra—a lot. But I am not up to committed relationships. I recently got divorced, and my daughters are my top priority."

I felt a little hurt because I liked him. We women get attached right after or as soon as we sleep with a man and even more so if it was great sex.

"I understand. I think it will be better for both of us to go separate ways," I suggested.

I had not called him back since that night. A year later, I got a text from him asking me out. I was not interested. *If he let me go then, why get back together now?* I believe in one theory: if it did not work out the first time, what makes you think that it will work out the second time? Latin men are great lovers, but I can't deal with baby mama dramas, and I do not have time for this crap. Some Latin men consider dramatic and jealous women very attractive. I have observed a fact about Latin men sticking to their Latin women. In my opinion, it is a perfect compatibility: the same food, the same language, the same culture, and the same sense of humor. I bet they speak Spanish when they make love.

What not to date:

- Men who want to get laid but with no commitment
- Men whose ex-wife is a stalker with baby mama drama
- Men who try to come back to you after they let you go

CHAPTER 11

Ivy League Grad and His Unbuttoned Briefs

As MY JOB WAS TO bring business to the hotel, I was entertaining a top client at our gorgeous hotel, and the crowd was awesome. The DJ was spinning cool vibes and encouraging "slip and slide, sip and swim." I, Brooks, and her two friends were sipping cosmos, and suddenly we saw three guys approaching us. They were walking like *Entourage*—with the exception that these guys were way better-looking than the actors in *Entourage*. Impressing me is hard. But Andrew's charming smile and courage to approach me impressed me. Our eyes met, his eyes radiated intelligence, and my eyes reflected flicker.

"Can I buy you a drink? What would you prefer?" he said in a squeaky voice. My smile faded with disappointment.

"You have to buy drinks for my friends," I politely requested.

"I am Andrew," Squeaky Voice introduced himself.

I am too picky, but despite his annoyingly squeaky voice, Andrew was like a walking encyclopedia. He was everything that I was looking for in a man: Ivy League grad, good looks, very smart, a profound sense of humor. Andrew was charming, and he had approached me the moment he saw me. He and his friends made us laugh the entire evening.

My clients went back to the hotel. Andrew offered to take me for a ride in his Lamborghini. It was a gorgeous car, matte black, and the roaring sound of it made me wet.

"I want to take you for a drive around Miami."

"I dreamed about it, but in my own Lamborghini."

"Consider it done. It is yours. You want to drive my gorgeous baby, beautiful?"

"Let's make love—three of us: you, me, and her."

The drive was scenic and breathtaking. It was almost sunrise. A day was waking up, and sunbeams were touching the faces, trees, and flowers. The breeze was wrapping us so affectionately; roaring beauty and him holding my hand was just a dream come true. Beautiful and intelligent people with good hearts were having the time of their lives.

His place was in a prestigious area in Key Biscayne, Miami. He owned a two-bedroom condo facing the bay, very spacious and decorated tastefully.

"Would you like something to drink, sweetie?"

"What do you have?"

"Belvedere, Grey Goose, Black Label, Veuve Clicquot. Should I keep going?"

"Veuve Clicquot, please!" I raised my hands and laughed lightly. "Do you speak French?"

"I speak French fluently." Andrew kept surprising me every minute.

Nothing is more romantic than an American speaking French. We were talking about what happened after the USSR disintegrated, the war in Chechnya, the Serbian war, *The Art of War*, the USA and Israel, and the Israel and Palestine.

He was undressing me slowly, but he would not let me undress him. I liked this kind of foreplay. He finally undressed, and I saw him in cute little briefs with cute buttons with smiley emoji and printed red lips.

"This is the only thing my ex-girlfriend gave me for Valentine's Day."

I was wondering why his ex-girlfriend left him. I do not like asking the reason why a previous relationship did not work out. I consider it as a private and personal question to ask for the first date.

We were kissing and caressing each other, and the moment I was reaching out to take his briefs off him, he slapped my hands. *Hmm. Should I play some game with him? Beg him?*

"Can I please see and feel him? I am dying to see the thick and fat sausage." I was speaking out of my nostrils. Talking out of nostrils is considered sexy in some Asian countries, but it's annoying to me. Well, that excessive nasality worked on Andrew. He unbuttoned his briefs, and there it was: tiny boy Andy and his little balls. I think a dwarf has a bigger penis and balls than Andrew. I could hardly hold my laugh, but I needed to understand him.

While we were making love, I felt like he was fingering me. It was sad and funny at the same time. He was a successful Ivy League grad who was good-looking but with a tiny wiener and a high-pitched voice.

Later, we were in his bed, but he would not shut up and stop talking about politics and global history. And he would not take off his briefs. Perhaps he imagined his briefs covering his imaginary bigger balls. However, I could see the tiniest balls and the smallest woodpecker. Andrew was so commanding in bed, and he sounded like Lieutenant Dan in the *Forrest Gump* movie with a high-pitched voice.

"Arch your back more. Bend over more!" His squeaky voice ruined it.

I could not understand how it would help him grow his penis larger if I kept bending over. Half an hour later, his small boy felt like a pinch. I am curious about the correlation between high-pitched voices and the male reproductive system. I think low-pitched voices are more masculine and have more sperm activity.

Here are my choices:

Ivy League, highly intelligent, attractive, good personality but with the tiniest balls, a small penis, and a squeaky voice

Hot model, broke ass, smart, hung 24-7, user, angry all the time

Low-pitched voice and the best sex but immature

My choice: none of the above in normal circumstances. If I ended up on an isolated island, I would choose number 3. A squeaky voice with a short and thin sausage is the worst combination. Hopefully Andrew can fix his voice. I am certain he can't get a bigger penis. It's so unfair and sad.

What not to date:

- A man who wears buttoned briefs all the time in the bedroom
- A man who does not shut up while having sex
- A man who has the tiniest penis. This problem is not solvable.

CHAPTER 12

Stinky Stigmata

DMITRI WAS HIS NAME. HE was a tall and handsome Eastern European who was a personal driver to celebrities who'd visit Miami. He was on his schedule. We grabbed drinks at Novecento; he was instantly into me. I was a little bit cautious. I don't trust Eastern Europeans for a few reasons: their political situations and their tendency to be people who blame and hate the Soviet Union regime and Russians. Even the younger generation of Eastern Europeans has such hatred toward Russians. I consider it as ignorance. The Generation Y of Eastern Europe must accept that they would not have prospered on their own between 1970 and 1990. It is a fact that the former Yugoslavia was the worst of all; they never had intellectual power. Maybe hacking was their calling.

Why did the European Union and International Monetary Fund bail out these bankrupted countries? As a matter of fact, for centuries, British, Germans, Scandinavians have been more progressive and still are. They excelled in science and craftsmanship in the seventeenth century. Frankly speaking, EU does not need to drag and enable them. During the Soviet Union era, countries like Romania and the former Yugoslavia did not advance in anything. Every country should have the intellectual power, scientific advancements, and intelligence to be accepted and to take advantage of the EU.

I had broken up with Narcissistic Model and Baby Mama Drama. I cleared my head and tried to get a fresher perspective on my personal life. I wanted to have fun with Dmitri and have sex with no strings attached. It is crucial for women my age to maintain a healthy sexual life. It was too hot in his car, and the Serbian folk music playing in his car made me feel unsexy. He was one of those immigrants who would never get adjusted and be open-minded. He would listen only to his folk and modern music originated by Serbian artists. Dimitri was not trying American burgers, Italian pasta, Japanese sushi, Colombian arepas, Peruvian ceviche but would talk about how great Serbia was and how delicious Serbian food was. He showed me images of Serbian nature and told me how bad he wanted to go back. I say it was bullcrap. I thought, *If you hate the USA, no one is holding you here. Please leave.* I did not like his hatred toward Americans.

After a few dates, I found it weird and unmanly of him not to invite me to his place. The explanation was that he shared a studio with his friend. His studio was so small that he had legs hanging one foot away from the entrance door. He was thirty-seven years old. We did not get down that night. The biggest turn-off was he was sweating profusely. I do not think he used a deodorant. Or perhaps he did not take a shower religiously, or he ate food that caused the smell. When sweat was coming out through his skin pores, it touched and reached my sensitive sense of smell. Body smell is important. I have keen sense of smell, like a dog.

"Have you seen *The Exorcist*?"

"No, I do not waste my time watching useless movies about exorcism, stigmatism, and all movies of that nature. I do not believe in that kind of crap. I believe in science," I proudly stated.

Dmitri's facial expression changed to a judgmental look, and he said, "Oh yeah? You are a science person. How do you explain what had happened to me when I was at a Catholic church in Belgrade? There is a pastor who has a magical power to heal people." Dimitri got really worked up.

"I don't believe in this bullcrap. It is all staged to get money out of stupid and uneducated people. Religion manipulates the weak and uneducated masses."

With great enthusiasm and confidence, Dmitri set out to prove me wrong. I felt like I could read his dark and exorcism-infested mind. "My entire family was at the church attending Sunday service. The pastor asked two ladies to come up closer to him. One of them was in a wheelchair. It was a sad story. She was in a car accident and got paralyzed from the waist down. Another lady was carrying a cane, and she came with hope to find a cure from the pastor. The pastor addressed the woman in a wheelchair, 'Try to get out of the seat and walk toward me, and I am empowering you with the force of God, and I command you to walk. You can walk now.' But the woman could not move from her wheelchair. The pastor summarized his decision to the entire church: 'You are not worthy of a chance because you were a prostitute in the past, and you are not going to get on your feet ever again.' Everyone in the church sighed deep and agreed with his statement."

"Do not tell me you believe this?" I asked, irritated.

"The other lady could walk straight without the cane right after the pastor touched her and took away the cane. It is true. How would you explain since you are a science person?" said Dmitri with his stupid-looking eyes.

He continued, "My car CD was not working. I took it to the pastor, and he blessed it. Since then, it has been almost two years, and the same CD still works."

"Don't you think it was a technical issue and has nothing to do with God's power?" I questioned him.

"No. Your scientific mindset is bullshit. To convince you, Alexandra, and make you believe in exorcism, I have seen a person bleeding at the places similar to crucified Christ was bleeding."

"I say it is bullshit. I do not want to get annoyed more and aggravate myself. It does not make any sense. I think it is all made up to manipulate the masses. The churches manipulate uneducated, pessimistic, purposeless, and weak people. The pastors make millions by stealing money from people and not paying taxes. They know whoever comes to churches is already in trouble. It is easier to manipulate weak and uneducated people. I am getting tired. Can you please leave now? I need to get a good sleep. Tomorrow is going to be a very long and tough day for me. And before you leave, how do you explain to me the priests molesting kids, taking advantage of the kids whose parents are abusive alcoholics and drug addicts?" I asked him to make him feel like a fuckwit.

Dmitri could not say a word. So two days later, this dumb fuck called me saying he wanted to see me. I told him I was not interested anymore and asked him politely not to call me anymore. He did not get why I did not want to see him. Maybe he should find someone who was into stigmata. I just couldn't deal with his stupidity and bad body odor. I do not think anyone can unless the other person does not also smell right. Dmitri smelled like moldy cheese with sweat.

What not to date:

- Men with a bad body smell
- Men who are stigmatic and obviously do not believe in science
- Men who listen to their folk music in the cars all the time
- Men who do not adjust to the country they live in
- Men who are ignorant

CHAPTER 13

Age Ain't Nothing but a Number

HERE'S MY OBSERVATION ABOUT FACEBOOK maniacs: there are two types of profiles and personalities on social media. The first one, I call them Fake Happy. They are mainly making stuff up, posting happy images, eating at expensive restaurants, or taking selfies with the hottest friends and guys to prove to everyone else that they are the happy, glamorous, and fancy. But deep down inside, they are empty, lonely, and not content with themselves. It is the most unsociable and impersonal friendship that is out there.

The second type I call Inspirational Vomit—those who consistently post inspirational quotes, quotes about life, happiness, and love. They do so with intentions of making an impression of a smart person and inspirational character. I say it is annoying.

The funny fact is, when Happy Fake or Inspirational Vomit responds to highly original quotes and images, they post and react with emoji. They can't elaborate on any subject or quote they post. I find the overuse of all emoji to be degrading. Both do not know how to articulate thoughts and express emotions.

It was a Saturday night, and I was staying in drinking my red wine. I came across an interesting profile: an intelligent man named John Smith. What a typical American name. His

Facebook profile was full of brainyquotes.com. What turned me on about John was our conversation about Ayn Rand's *The Fountainhead,* the most amazing and inspiring book about a man of independence and integrity, mover and shaker, and individualism against collectivism. I reread this book twice, lingering on the statement "The impassioned faith in your individuality." Each time I read this fantastic book, I had discovered that I could not agree more with this statement and the idea of a gifted, visionary sense of individuality. I am passionate about hotels and love what I do. I possess great knowledge and experience, very much driven by inexhaustible energy and the desire to make a guest's stay the most enjoyable and memorable. *The Fountainhead's* main character inspired and helped me fight and overcome my fears. The main character went through rough times and became penniless, but he was a very strong and visionary architect who had put his name on one of the most famous and best buildings in a big city. I strongly believe that every person has a gift or talent. It takes the right people, company, and education to achieve and realize your big dreams. My dream is to launch my own hotel brand in the near future. I am not just dreaming of making it a reality; I am working hard on the business plan and more these days after my regular work hours. Every time I get an aha moment, I get convinced that my dream will become a reality soon.

But back to John Smith. Another attractive thing about him was how hilarious he was. He and I were cracking up talking about Seth MacFarlane. If you make me laugh, it turns me on. I love a guy with a profound sense of humor, and if he makes me laugh, I am all his, from head to toe.

"Wow, I am very impressed by your knowledge and English, Alexandra. How is it possible that a smart and attractive girl like you is single?" said John, puzzled.

Honestly I hate questions that require a response that will lead to selling myself and bragging about my achievements and success story. After seven days of intelligent conversations, I wanted to meet him.

In my imagination, John Smith was tall, good-looking, entertaining, and I would be completely smitten by him. I was sitting in the lounge at a bar. And here he came: overweight, twenty years older, and with thick glasses—looking like *The Nutty Professor* but Caucasian. I could not believe my eyes. He lied about his age. It was another stupid move that guys do. He was very nervous and was biting his nails, which I find very childish and indicative of an oral hygiene problem. Guys who bite their nails off, to me, are nervous, stingy, or insecure. Overall, his appearance left not much to be desired. We were in a Mexican restaurant. John finished his food so fast and already preyed on my food:

"Mexican food is so delicious that I can't get enough. Can I taste a little bit of your guacamole and quesadilla?"

I saw him salivating over my quesadillas. I called him Fat Bastard since he resembled Fat Bastard from *Austin Powers: The Spy Who Shagged Me*. The only thing that was missing was him saying, "Shall we shag now, or shall we shag later? Behave, baby."

"You are pretty, and you look so young! I would not give you more than thirty years." He was smacking his food.

I couldn't say the same thing about him. It almost came out of my mouth. Instead, I politely answered, "Thank you." I lost my appetite when I saw his sausage fingers crawling on my food. "Please go ahead and finish the quesadilla."

I was looking at him and thinking, *What the hell was he thinking about when he posted his old pictures? That was so wrong of him. Or was it a sick and spooky game? And he keeps smacking his lips while eating my food!*

It was the worst date ever. I had to leave half an hour later faking an emergency. The emergency was sausage fingers that crawled on my paid food. *Let me get the hell out of here!*

Who hides their age? We are always conscious about it, but some people get some plastic surgery. Yet when they smile, their skin is so tight that it makes them look unattractive. We should take diligent care of ourselves, our minds and bodies, always. There is this saying by Anton Chekhov: "Everything must be beautiful in person: body, mind and soul."

What not to date:

- Men who do not take care of themselves
- Men who eat your food at the first date
- Men who do not have self-respect
- Men who post their old pictures on e-dating sites

CHAPTER 14

Open Relationships and 21 Movie Characters

MY PASSION FOR HOTEL BUSINESS brought me to the greatest country in the world. I am happy with my current job.

It was my third hotel opening. The hotel preopening is a fantastic experience—the most intense and challenging but also the most rewarding. During the interview process, all the candidates are being nice and saying things you want to hear, saying how committed they are and how they will not let you down.

We hired an interesting character. His name was Stanley. He wore XXX-large suspenders; his belly was round like a ball that it was bouncing off every table, corner, and food plate. His wife turned out to be crazy jealous and was FaceTiming every hour while he was at work. His wife was retired and had nothing to do all day long. I would have suggested her to keep her mind busy. No one at work would lay eyes on him. He had such a big belly that she would have to lift it up and look for his buried penis. I wondered about what being fat does to a penis. For every thirty to fifty excess weight, men lose one inch of visible penis. I hope losing weight would motivate not only Stanley but also other overweight men. Women look good with curves and some cute fat, but men do not. Can you imagine how male fat asses look in bed?

I got lucky because I got a very good team. As for me, I was excited to develop the sales and marketing plan, attracting the right clients to the hotel and creating marketing events. The entire eleven months were very intense: developing the brand concept, working on marketing collateral and sales collateral, traveling and attending networking events, and overseeing the sales, marketing, and revenue managers. I loved every minute of it.

Two months prior to the hotel opening, I got a lot on my plate. I was responsible for orchestrating the event and doing the presentation of the brand-new hotel in the US followed by the welcome reception. The CEO expected a terrific crowd, as investors, lawyers, financial and banking industry leaders, and potential vendors would be all gathered there that night. We are in the business of making people happy: welcoming and greeting, getting the rooms and all requests delivered, sending the birthday cakes and hangover kits for the bachelors and bachelorettes, and helping a wealthy guy find his Rolex watch that got stolen by a prostitute. That is why I love the hotel business. Every day is different, and always something good and eventful takes place only at a hotel. Most hoteliers are good, happy, and outgoing people.

After the welcome reception, I had a bad hangover. I wanted eggs, bacon, and tomato juice to quench my thirst. I walked over to the local Whole Foods. I did not take off my sunglasses. I was wearing all-black clothes and red shoes, and I took a seat in a very lonely corner. Bummer. It was 10:30 a.m., and no breakfast was served at Whole Foods. I got chicken noodle soup and half a sandwich. I was squeezing a spicy sauce in my soup, quenching my thirst with icy Perrier, and enjoying the moment. Suddenly I heard someone say, "Soup, sunglasses are on, Prada shoes, sparkling water. It must have been a rough night."

I was looking through my sunglasses and saw a good-looking man sitting next to me and said, "Very rough night indeed—good times, business dinner, drinks. Curing my hangover now. No judging, please." I rolled my eyes.

"No judging at all. I am Jonathan. What do you do for a living?"

"Alexandra, hotel sales and marketing director."

"It is very refreshing to meet an independent woman these days. Women in Miami are looking for rich and wealthy only."

"What do you do for a living?" I asked him to carry a conversation. At that moment, I did not care about anything but curing my hangover.

"Different things: real estate and corporate positions at a freight company."

"Cool. I got to go back to work." I was in a hurry.

"How can we keep in touch?"

"Perhaps a phone number would help," I made fun of him.

Jonathan smiled at me. The very next day, Jonathan invited me for a coffee. We had an enjoyable conversation. We laughed and shared interesting stories.

That same day, right after work, I went to Target; and on the way out, my phone rang. "You look good in white shorts and wedges. Come back. I am right behind you." Jonathan smiled over the phone.

"Are you stalking me?" I was flirting.

"Wow, it must be destiny. We came across each other twice for the past two days."

"I do not believe it is destiny. You probably live around here in this neighborhood. The chances of bumping into each other are high. The behavioral pattern of professionals is identical. Picking up groceries after work can very much happen at the same time." I was being a smart-ass.

He was laughing. "You are right. Can I give you a ride home?"

"No, thanks. I live around the corner."

"You want to meet tomorrow for lunch?" charming Jonathan asked.

"Yes, Friday lunch sounds great."

I was excited to meet up with Jonathan because he seemed different than the other guys I had dated. The guys in the past wanted to get in bed. It was refreshing and not imposing to not have sex but get to know each other and take it very slowly.

"Do you have any weekend plans?" I asked him with the hope we could spend time on the beach together.

"Yes, my parents are in town from Italy. I am going to take them out for dinner and show them Miami."

"Nice. Sounds amazing!"

Over the weekend, we exchanged flirtatious texts, which made me feel great and hopeful. I liked the way it was going.

On Monday morning, at 10:00 a.m., I got a text and a lunch invite.

"I got divorced twice. My ex-wife was addicted to alcohol and drugs. I had to get out of the marriage. Otherwise, it would have destroyed me. I lost a lot of money. She was going to rehab and taking all hard-core antidepressants," said Jonathan with a deep sigh.

"I feel you. I went through the same with my ex. Rehabs do not work. It is the Brainchild of all pharmaceutical companies that get you dependent on antidepressants. All antidepressants have side effects that can have adverse reactions. For those who are reliant on drugs, it is a done deal. Weak people with no strong willpower can't get out of it. They will blame everyone—dwell on their childhood and how they got bullied or heartbroken by their first love."

"Alexandra, you get me. Thank you so much, Whole Foods, for bringing such a good and understanding friend."

"Do you want to take any pictures with me?" I asked him.

"I do not take good pictures in general. Would you want to see the pictures of my place?" he delicately turned down my offer.

Shuffling through all the images, I thought, *Wait, his bedroom, with a tray and two wine glasses.* "Do you live with someone, Jonathan?"

"Wow, you are smart, Alexandra!"

"Do you? And is this why you couldn't see me over the weekend?" I was dying to hear his answer.

"I want to be honest with you. I am living with a woman, and we both have an open relationship."

"Really? Do you think any woman in this overpopulated city where good men are in high demand would be okay with an open relationship?" I asked him with indifference in my voice.

"Yes, I got lucky. She is an independent woman, and she's okay with open relationships."

"Thank you for lunch." I could not get out of his car faster. I was in shock over this guy who had made a perfect impression on me. He could carry an interesting conversation and was very respectful, funny, and good-looking. I thought, *What is wrong with me? Do I attract the worst kinds of guys? Does it say on my forehead "Date Alexandra if you are a jerk"?* On a positive note, at least I was getting better with cracking the asshole codes and profiling bad guys.

On Friday night, my friends and coworkers gathered for happy hour after work. I glanced at my phone and saw a text from Jerk Jonathan: "You do not miss me?"

"It was great meeting you, but I am not interested in seeing someone, especially one who lives with his girlfriend. Please refrain from calling me or contacting me in the future."

"Alexandra, I was never attracted to you in the first place. Never wanted to have sex with you. You are not my type. Just wanted to be a friend and learn about the hotel business. I already deleted you from LinkedIn." He hit low.

"I am crying a river."

My girlfriends and I had gathered for drinks to talk about guys and our dating lives. I spoke of the asshole, and one of my friends started screaming and asking me what he looked like. I could not get why she was so antsy and eager to know what this asshole looked like and what his name was. I showed her his Facebook profile picture, and she jumped out of her chair and screamed, "That is the same guy who approached me at Whole Foods a few weeks ago!"

During lunch hours, Whole Foods Downtown gets infested with professional employees, comparable to Downtown NYC or Tokyo. All you see is men dressed up in expensive suits. I guarantee you, Jonathan went there during lunch hours and fished for successful women. Downtown and Brickell is the Southern Wall Street. You can meet successful women at the right location and at networking events. Jonathan still hoped to meet and become friends with an independent woman who would not mind dealing with his open relationship bullcrap.

That weekend, I went to Starbucks to finish my sales budget. I heard someone say, "You must be very smart, and you must hold a very high position or have your own business."

I looked to my left and saw a guy in his late twenties, skinny with a light beard. His name was Sam. He played poker with his clients' money and shared fifty-fifty profits and traveled extensively to Las Vegas.

"The movie *21* is based on my life story," said Sam with a big smile.

The plot revolves around a character named Ben Campbell, a brilliant student at MIT who needs some quick cash to pay his tuition fees. So he joins a group of students who, under the leadership of their professor, use their math skills to win big in Las Vegas."

Sam proudly showed off all the images he had with celebrities with whom he made millions. I was skeptical about the pictures knowing they could be faked and photoshopped.

"I have to leave now because my friend is picking me up."

"Wait, Alexandra. Can I have your number? You are going to miss an opportunity of making $5,000 in one day," he said at the end of the conversation.

"I am not that stupid to trust you." I laughed at him.

What not to date:

- Men who claim to have open relationships and their living girlfriends are fine with the arrangement
- Men who invite you for lunch, not dinners
- Men who does not pick up their phones over the weekends
- Men who impersonate actors

CHAPTER 15

Let Us Go Dutch!

AFTER DATING LONG-DISTANCE FOR A year, one of my friends' best friends decided to move in with her first American boyfriend. He was an average Joe, and sadly, she fell in love with him. Her name was Alexandra, and his name was Ben. He would never even pay for her ticket or even lunch, but he wanted to see her every month.

Alexandra left Miami for a hole-in-the-wall town in Wisconsin. Before they decided to move in together, he made the rule to split all the bills fifty-fifty. Ben got paid twice as much, but he still wanted her to pay fifty-fifty. They moved in together. That penny-pincher flew by airplane. She drove in her beat-up car. We suggested to Alexandra to sell her car and buy a new one or use his car. Her new job was just ten minutes away from their place. They could have one car. But Ben asked her to split the gas and monthly insurance plan.

The last rule killed me, and I lost respect for Ben forever. Both would split sixty-forty for grocery shopping. Apparently, Ben ate more steak. Later, he calculated that the large quantity of fruit she ate cost the same as few extra pounds of steak he ate. I called him Tightwad.

During one of her farewell dinners, we were at a Japanese restaurant. The restaurant had a loyalty card program. As the restau-

rant business was fiercely competitive, they came up with a cumu-
lative points system. The more you'd eat, the more points you'd
get. The waitress brought the bill. It was thirty-five dollars total for
four people, and he would not even look at the bill. He made her
pay for the sushi with the rewards card. Stingy Benny flew in and
stayed at the cheapest hotel he could afford. I won't fuck a miser
Scrooge even if they are amazing lovers. But I wondered how tightfisted he must had been during sex? Stingy people do not become
generous overnight. It might look and go like this: Penny-pincher
wants you to come good, and in exchange, you must make him
equally come good. He goes down on you if you go down on him.

It is a well-known fact that every guy on this six-billion
overpopulated planet wants to have a threesome and anal sex.
If I were her, I would agree under one condition: sex with two
guys equals sex with two girls. When it'd be time for grocery
shopping, I would tell this tightfisted jerk, "How about you pay
all the bills so that you can have threesome every weekend?"

His answer would be, "No, we pay fifty-fifty, and let us not
mix business with pleasure."

I heard that last Christmas, she bought him a symbolic
and very expensive watch. Stingy Ass got her a twenty-dollar
bracelet from Ross. For Christmas, people make an exception
and buy meaningful gifts.

Since we are talking about tightwads and sex addicts, I will
share a date I had recently. His name was Juan. He approached
me in Starbucks. "You are interesting, and I would love to get
to know you."

I had never been asked out in Starbucks, as it is a place for
nerds and business coffee breaks.

Juan was running fifteen minutes late; I guess it is typical
of Miamians. In my opinion, being late is rude and inconsider-
ate of others' time.

"You look mysterious in red, Alexandra. The black hair, the color of your skin, and your sexy face compliment your dress." He gazed at me. "What is your type, Alexandra? Do you like to be scratched or bitten, and do you scream when you come?"

I laughed so loud that everyone in the restaurant looked at us and gave us a judgmental look.

"Do you like to be penetrated deep? Do you squirt? I fucked a Thai girl once. Did you ever have a threesome?" This obnoxious fifty-year-old fart was drooling all over me.

I decided to play the same game with the pervert. "I love sex and all positions and types," I responded in a nasally voice.

"I heard Asian women are great in sex, but you are Russian Korean," Juan tried to provoke me.

"Everyone is the same, no difference."

"Do you know what we Latin Miamians call gold diggers? I hate gold diggers to their guts," said Juan.

Mr. Repugnant Juan did not listen to what I said. I wanted to get out of there. "No, I have no clue. Enlarge my vocabulary." I sounded indifferent.

"We say they have got a calculator in their pussy."

"It sounds vulgar. I have never heard of it." I felt a bad taste in my mouth. I was disgusted by his obnoxious comments.

"If I know that the whore has a calculator in her pussy, I just destroy her pussy so that she can't calculate any money after me with other guys," said Juan.

"Wow, you are quite respectful of women. So you got divorced after three years of marriage. What happened?" I asked to annoy him with my questions.

"She makes more money than me. She is becoming a feminist. I hate feminists."

"You should be proud to be with a successful woman. You are a misogynist," I concluded.

The waiter came back twice. Juan could not make up his mind because he was calculating how much it would cost him. He was a unique case: sex maniac, misogynist, and tightfisted. Their behavior is very predictable. What causes misogyny are women's rejection, being a mama's boy, and trust issues. And they think they can fuck any woman they want. I was looking at him and observing his thought process in his eyes. Eyes never lie. Juan's process of reflection flowed like this: "I like her. We can start with the salad and appetizer to share, and I will exhaust the waitress with all the combo and special of the night." I was so right about Juan's thinking.

"You used to have a sushi roll that has salmon, tuna, eel, and whitefish at a lower price," Nervous Juan said.

"It must be an emperor roll," the waitress responded politely.

"Let me have the sashimi sample, but wait, how many pieces are there?"

"It is twenty-two dollars."

"No, let me have the salad, edamame, and special roll for $6.75," Stingy Nerves asked.

My Russian friend texted me asking about my date with Juan. I texted her back in Russian: *jadniy svoloch*, which translates as "stingy bastard."

"What does your text mean?" Juan asked.

"I meant to send the text to my Russian friend. The text means you are generous and cool." I burst out laughing.

"It sounds so sexy. Hmm. I will save it." Sex Maniac Juan was salivating. "I want to have sex with you tonight." He was rubbing my legs.

I slapped his hands. Here was the continuation of his thought process: "The restaurant closes at eleven p.m., which is in an hour and a half. Half an hour is enough to have one drink or two glasses of the cheapest wine and not too much food as the kitchen closes at ten p.m. I am so smart that I made the dinner reservation one hour before the kitchen closes."

"Let me just have tuna and salmon roll." I rolled my eyes.

He kept thinking how much the dinner would cost him if he would not get laid tonight. I left right after he paid the bill.

A few days later, Juan texted me.

"Would you be interested in working with me?" Juan asked.

"Who is it?" I got puzzled.

"*Jadniy svoloch* (stingy bastard)," deluded Juan responded.

"No way. Working with you would be a great case of sexual harassment. I do not sleep with coworkers. It is against my principles to sleep with my boss."

I can't fuck stingy, obnoxious, women-hating, disrespectful sex addicts. Good luck to Juan! I hope he finds a nymphomaniac and an offensive gold digger.

What not to date:

- Men who want to split fifty-fifty on everything, including sex
- Men who have sex with their employees
- Men who never listen
- Men who are disrespectful to women

CHAPTER 16

From Russia with Love

THIS IS MY OPINION ABOUT mixed couples: mixed-race babies make cute babies. Koreans like to stick to their own. All my cousins and brothers are married to Koreans only. We in the family did not mix with any other races and nationalities. It was during 1990–1996. I remember when I was in my early twenties dating a Ukrainian guy; I got judged by all the grandmothers and aunts of the entire Korean community. I also dated a Korean guy, but he was so mean to me. He was a very arrogant and stuck-up asshole because I lived in the hostels in Uzbekistan, which were not as luxurious as the hostels here in the USA—no individual bathrooms and showers and kitchens. Everything was meant to be shared. But for me, it was awesome and something to remember and laugh about.

Back in the '90s, they used to say that Korean women made better wives than Russians. The difference between the two was that Korean women knew how to take care of their husbands and kids. They would strive to create great times and plenty of true family quality time, and they genuinely cared about one another. I remember my mom would not eat dinner without my dad. She would wait for him to come home, greet him, and kiss him. We had two sets of side dishes and soups, and main dishes always were served individually. No one would be digging in your bowl. A separate set of side dishes was set up for Dad.

Times have changed, and anyone can date whomever they want. They can marry whom they want. Korean or Russian is all the same. The traditions are not as they used to be. After I dated American, Latin, British, Black, French, and Eastern European boys, I realized that meeting someone from the same country is better and closer to my roots. Two people from the same country can understand each other. You have the same sense of humor, enjoy the same dishes, and watch classic movies from your country when the mood strikes you both at the same time. Most importantly, you speak the same language.

All the above speculations would justify why I was with this Russian guy then. I met a Russian guy online. We clicked instantly, had a nice dinner, and ended up at my place a few hours later. His name was Boris—good looking, tall, blue-eyed with dark-brown hair, and with a very heavy Russian mixed with Serbian accent. Nothing was wrong with that. Every accent is charming. He began to undress me and walk toward my bedroom. He would kiss me all over my body, but two minutes later, he would come. I thought to myself, *What a quick-stainer.* I was nice and said, "It is okay. It happens."

"Honey, I want you to meet my mom," Boris said after the second date and sex we had.

"After two dates? Don't you think it is too fast?"

"I like you, and I know my mom would love you."

His mom, you could tell, was one of those who'd get jealous but act like they were the nicest. She liked me right away and approved her son's choice.

"Tonight we will go out with my friends and cheer you up."

"Sounds good. I am excited!"

"We are going to have fun!"

"Superb!"

After two dates, I started seeing a couple of Boris's shirts in my closet. I loved to smell his shirts. A week later, he brought his turntables to my second bedroom, which was empty anyway. I felt we would be good together. Two weeks of dating with my hot Russian boyfriend, and we were living together. I cooked Russian dishes for him, and we went out with his friends occasionally. Everything was going fast and easy at the same time.

Work had been crazy busy and overwhelming: eighty to ninety hours a week, coordinating a photoshoot for straight eleven hours, steaming the curtains for the photoshoot, developing intelligent reporting system for the CEO, pushing the sales team to get the business, pursuing group business, visiting all my corporate clients, going to sites and dinners with prospective clients, hosting a breakfast with Greater Miami Convention and Visitors Bureau, working with the revenue manager on optimizing revenues and implementing digital marketing strategies, to name a few. I love what I do. That is what makes me keep going to get creative and become better. But it physically took its toll on my body to the extent that I started to burn out.

Unfortunately, recognition was not in the mind and vocabulary of my boss. And as the pressure always came from the upper management, my team and I were feeling more pressure but were less appreciated. It takes approximately six months to gain higher occupancy and get loyal clients, provided that the brand-new hotel delivers an impeccable service, has personalized and customized marketing campaigns, and the room quality is impressive with a sleek, modern design. The tension had risen to the highest degree of temperature between my boss and myself. I decided to resign. It was sad for me to say goodbye to my team. It was unfair because I was put down and disrespected for all the work I had done. Why should I waste my nervous cells and fight battles with unintelligent and mean people? I always wonder why and how these heartless people get the top position.

I always get something great and worthy. The next hotel I will work at must be American and well-structured. And being on edge is what makes me better and relentless. I do not take shit from anyone, especially from cynical, rotten, incompetent Ruthless Frauds. I saw a little twinge of pleasure in Ruthless Fraud's eyes when I resigned. What I had gained was profound experience. I won intellectual battles, earned brownie points from the CEO of the company, and my team respected me.

For the past eleven months, I felt humiliated and disrespected, and I never got appreciated and recognized. The last drop that exasperated my patience was her mocking of my cultural background in front of everyone. I wore a silk Chinese dress because I wanted to. Female Ruthless Fraud turned around and, with a smirk on her face, said, "You are in the wrong hotel. You do not belong here. We are a Latin American brand, and you look like you belong to a Mandarin Oriental hotel."

I threw it right back at her and, with a smile, said, "It is getting quite boring here. I decided to spice things up, Asian style."

She did not even realize her act made her look stupid and unprofessional. Every hotel has that one person who disrupts the dynamics and ruins the happiness of the rest, and there is always a Snitch Bitch attached to a Ruthless Fraud. In life, the older you get, the less good friends you find. I am fortunate to have great friends, except for one Ukrainian who turned into a Snitch Bitch. I eliminated her from my friends' zone and put her on my shit list. I knew her for a couple years; we used to work together at a boutique hotel in South Beach. I joined this brand-new hotel, fought for her, and brought her on board, and she happened to be my next-door neighbor. What a coincidence! I thought at that time that our friendship would last long-term.

Since the day I quit, Snitch Bitch got very distant from me. I let it go until one night. One Friday night, my Russian boy toy and I were making noises and moaning when building security knocked at my door due to a noise complaint from her. At that moment, it just hit me that it was her who snitched about me and gave the printed pages of my social media comments about my resignation and my advice on how to teach Ruthless Frauds a lesson in life. After I resigned from this last hotel, my ex-boss posted my job position on her personal Facebook and tagged me. We all know that it is a small world, especially in the Miami hotel industry. I got tons of messages and got humiliated through social media by Ruthless Fraud. My former colleagues thought that I had been fired. I went back and made a statement about my willful resignation, not firing. I made comments about people with evil hearts. That spurred comments and reactions such as "Alexandra, you made the right decision. And whatever you choose to do, you will succeed! We are happy for you if you are happy about your decision!" Snitch Bitch left the printed pages with the above comments on the desk of the human resources director, walked me the next morning means as soon as director of sales leaves a two-week notice or resigns, director of human resources escorts you out so no clients' info is stolen.

If we were not neighbors and had I not got her a job, I wouldn't have known what kind of disgusting piece of shit she was. Snitch Bitch backstabbed me so that she could secure her position and gain the trust of Ruthless Fraud. The fear was that Ruthless Fraud would use my friendship with Snitch Bitch against her and cause her a job loss. The recent news was Female Ruthless Fraud and Snitch Bitch were best friends now. Snitch Bitch couldn't lose her job because she was a breadwinner and her pussy-wuss boyfriend did not work. He was like a house husband.

Frankly speaking, I always worked very well with male bosses. My previous male bosses often told me, "Alexandra, you are like a man. No emotions. You always get straight to the point and make rational decisions. You never flirt. You do not bullshit that other female partners or colleagues try to pull a feminism card. Feminists go above and beyond what is unnecessary."

"This is my take on feminism: too much of anything is bad. Diversity is healthy. Women in the USA have more rights than anywhere in the world. You find female CEOs and start-ups and business owners. I think the fanatic and strong feminists need to take a step back and learn how to balance, respect, and learn from their male bosses. If we women reset our minds to achieve greater results, it is business at the end of the day," I summarized my opinion.

My clear response earned me respect—the respect that I valued and reciprocated to my old GM who was my dearest and best GM and mentor and a wonderful person.

At the end of the day, women of all races, ethnicities, and religions want to be loved and want to be sexy and desirable to their men. There is this saying in Russian: "We men can't be without you as well as you women can't be without us." Nature dominates no matter what you think. We need to balance work and love life.

Boris had a lot of guy friends; they were either DJs, amateur artists, or Eastern European hackers. His female friends worked in real estate. I started noticing that Boris's female friends were too friendly with him. They called him in the middle of the night and asked him for help to move and hang TVs on the walls, which I found inappropriate.

Sandra invited us to her birthday dinner. We were at the adorable Italian restaurant Sylvano's. The food there is consistently good, and the staff is the friendliest of all seven hundred restaurants in Miami-Dade County. After dinner, we crashed the house party of some potheads from Egypt, Israel, Russia, Slovenia, Peru, Greece, and China. All of them got high except for me. Even Sandra's mom was smoking openly and wore a very provocative outfit. Her boobs were all over the place and said hi to Boris very enthusiastically. I got puzzled as to why a sixty-year-old woman was hanging out with us. Everything has its right time and place. Women in their late sixties should dress age-appropriately. She called herself a cool mom. It meant she dressed up too provocatively and age-inappropriately, made drinks for her children, acted like a young chick, and smoked her pot with her daughter's friends. I felt disgusted looking at her mom being all over Boris and how this hungry old duck was salivating over Boris. I flew out of there like a bullet from a rifle. Plus lame conversations about weed and all kinds of drugs were not interesting to me.

"Cool moms" never got it out of their systems or got knocked up earlier than they planned. They are dying to catch up with lost time and opportunities of being the center of attention. I would suggest finding your age group. I know I will be sixty years old one day, but I will know how to carry myself according to my age. Boris's female friends were weird and very loud. When women speak with nervousness in their voices, it reflects more about the lack of sex and attention from men.

It is a fact that children want to grow up faster, women get too panicky when they see the first wrinkle on their face, and teenagers are having sex. It is all wrong and unwise.

The very next morning, Boris called me at 10:00 a.m. from Sandra's phone. He stayed over at his other female Chinese friend's place. Boris confessed that there was something between them in the past. But he was not into her because her place was disorganized and dirty. When he called from Sandra's phone, I realized that he was so broke that he could not afford his own phone. But I understood his situation: he had just moved to Miami, and his mom had recently had a liver transplantation done. And it was just a temporary problem. I wanted to help him out.

"I want you to get pregnant. We will have beautiful kids," said Boris very confidently.

"It is a touching and very emotional subject for me, but we must be realistic. You do not have a job. I quit my job. There is no way we can have a baby now. We need to buy a house first and gain financial stability," I reacted.

"You worry too much. I will build the house with my bare hands. I will buy a megayacht, and we will be sailing in Biscayne Bay all the time," said deluded Boris as he stretched his thin hands up.

This time he lasted fifteen minutes. I was satisfied. But my moment of happiness was very short. Unfortunately, it was the only time he lasted longer than the usual three minutes. After two months of three-minute sex, flowers, and chocolate, the romance fever died off quickly. Another time, he had a put-'n'-shoot situation occurred, and we both looked at his stains and said, "These boys and girls are our kids." I smiled and thought, *It happened only with Boris. All his soldiers ended up backing up and ended up on the dry land—bedsheets. Interesting fact.*

In all honesty, I would not want to have a baby with a lazy and unemployed man with bad genetics. I started imagining how the sperm of potheads would reach my egg and lie on top of my ovaries:

> The vagina was like the canals in Venice; gondoliers should comfortably travel through. Boris smoked 24-7; his "gondoliers" were high off their asses. The gondoliers were

dressed in a striped blue shirt with bowler hat and were singing. But gondoliers singing would scare off all lovebirds. The gondoliers ended up on their own in the boats, but they were happy-high. They were swimming and rushing to lie on top of ovaries, and once they got high, they started walking in slow motion and their moves turned into turtle moves. One of 250,000 gondoliers resumed and proposed a toast in a drunk and high-from-weed voice: "Guys, I love and respect all of you. Go ahead and get to her before me. Next time, I will get there. For sure."

His voice sounded very chilled but with a strong Russian accent. Others were not moving their legs; they were sitting down on the floor and trying to take a hit and passing it around between fellow gondoliers. None of the gondoliers had made it to the finish line. All potheads were carefree. All lazy and high gondoliers didn't reach their final destination. They passed out and evaporated in the fog of weed.

To Boris, smoking pot and doing drugs were more important than taking care of a woman. Boris would spend his last twenty bucks to buy marijuana. I remember once I was craving for a Cuban sandwich. I asked him to buy me a sandwich. He came back with a bag of weed but no Cuban sandwich for me.

His sperms' behavior resembled his own; all Boris did was sleep till late and eat, smoke, and sleep. I found his style as a very primitive lifestyle. Oh, I forgot his three-minute sex he was so proud of.

I was about to leave to meet with my friends, and I heard a message on his phone. It was a Tinder message. Someone was texting him. I got mad, took a picture, and sent it to his other phone. Why would he have two phones? Now I understood why. One for a girlfriend whom his mom approved of, and the other phone was to meet other women. Well, his plan to live off me was not going to work out.

"What are you talking about, Alexandra? I deleted the app the day I met you," he said with nervousness in his voice.

"Hard to believe. Is this your phone? I am not stupid. I know how it works." I was furious.

"I am not talking to anyone now. I'm not cheating on you, and I don't steal from you. I pay for dinner once in a blue moon. I am a very good boyfriend."

"You should add to your description of your version the following: I do not have a job. I live off my girlfriend. This is my ideal setting: I wake up late, and I do not do shit. I am a quick-stainer, and I put-'n'-shoot and do not care if she is satisfied." All these thoughts crossed my mind. He was very selfish in bed.

"Do it yourself. I can't make you come. I do not know if you got hurt or something. It is damn difficult to make you come."

"Why is it that you come quick? Am I tight down there?" I asked him.

"No, you are not tight. That is why I come quickly."

"What about me? When are you going to make me come?" I was upset and humiliated.

"Three women proposed to me to marry them. They had orgasms at the snap of my fingers. I am trying, but it takes you forever. You just finish yourself, okay?"

Is there a name for women when the guys can't make them have an orgasm? For guys, it is "She gave him blue balls." If a man does not make her feel an orgasm, my Japanese friend suggested to refer to it as "He interrupted my cherry blossoming."

All unsuccessful and desperate attempts to have an orgasm made me invent a do-it-yourself kit, which consisted of an imaginary stallion, oil, glass of wine or cocktail, and both my hands. "Do it yourself" did not work for me. I was in the same bed lying down with a jobless pothead, quick-stainer, and dumbass with no bright future. All this called for an action, and the action was to kick him out.

"I know why you can't come and why you're always stressed out. It's because you are home all the time after you quit your job, and you should not have quit your job," said Boris, flossing his teeth in front of me.

"Are you serious? You live off me and do not pay for shit. Who are you to judge? You do not have room to say shit!" I yelled, knowing he hated it when I raised my voice at him.

Besides his put-'n'-shoot, Boris had unpleasant habits that turned into things that irritated the shit out of me:

- He left dirty tissue paper everywhere.
- He flossed his teeth in the kitchen while watching TV and in front of me. It is so disgusting and annoying to see a man flossing in front of you.
- He used Wite-Out and stroked a Wite-Out that we used for office supplies on the sneakers. The Wite-Out marks stained my beautiful wooden floor. Boris thought he was very smart about inventing a new way of cleaning his stupid white sneakers.
- He smacked his lips while eating.
- When he'd get angry and try to tell me how an accident happened, his skinny arms would move like windmills.

- He couldn't even articulate the situation but moved his skinny arms stupidly.

Being illiterate is like being the ugliest caveman of the twenty-first century. Slight or average accents are acceptable. But when Boris spoke English, he pronounced hard *r* like how Russians would pronounce hard rolling and roaring *r*. And he made goofy jokes; he irritated the shit out of me.

I realized the importance of a good upbringing and the genes of whom you date. Bad genes are hereditary through generations. I am sure it will come out and pass on third or fourth generations. I kicked him out. Without a single word, very prideful pothead and jobless DJ got kicked out of my house.

Just a week later, I was surfing online and saw his Facebook logged in on my laptop. He was already with some young Colombian girl. Colombian women in Miami are not going to go out with his broke and quick-stainer ass. And I found his Facebook Messenger's messages to his so-called "we are just friends." She was a French DJ who admired Boris. Two illiterate DJs dreaming to become the next DJ David Guetta deserved each other.

On a beautiful Thanksgiving morning, I felt like doing something good and necessary. I packed all his clothes in a small suitcase and took all the snacks out of my fridge and rolled my suitcase and walked four blocks to the bridge. I used to drive by that bridge and see homeless people on my way home. I always had it planned to bring them imperishable food and clothing. I gave them towels; a dozen of his cleaned and washed shirts, briefs, clothing, socks; and my old clothing. I felt an incredibly huge relief. Seeing their expressions and receiving genuine gratitude and a big hug was good for the soul.

Why did I not think about it before? Some women in a moment of rage and anger cut their boyfriends' shirts in half, throw them away, and burn their ex-boyfriends' clothes. I would recommend that you wash and fold them, pack the clothes into a suitcase, and give them away. Trust me, you will feel great.

What not to date:

- Illiterate, uneducated, lazy men
- Put-'n'-shooters
- Deluded potheads
- Arrogant DJs with no future
- Men who are too friendly with female friends and their pothead moms
- Mama's boys
- Freeloaders

CHAPTER 17

Return of the Athletic Sperm

IN MARCH 2017, TWO YEARS after we last saw each other, Chris called me. He wanted to see me. I wanted to see him badly too. I was in vulnerable situation at the time when I needed to make a right decision. To make some sort of income, I worked as a marketing consultant for a restaurant in an up-and-coming neighborhood in Miami. I got hired me with the hope that I would turn things around and make it a huge success. The first two months, the business was good.

I received an email from a famous fashion designer who paid for his birthday party. His birthday party was in three days. I found it strange that the fashion designer emailed from gmail. com and a Nigerian area code. To make a long story short, it turned out that the restaurant owners and their partner, a company that produced the credit cards, maxed out their fake credit cards by paying themselves to their own restaurant. It was a case of money laundering and stealing from the banks. Apparently, 60 percent of the restaurants in Miami close after a year or less of operating and few of the restaurants are used for money laundering. The restaurant owner treated his employees horribly, did not pay on time, and did drugs all the time. It was frustrating to all the workers and employees.

My sound mind and decision to report their asses spurred comments from my friends. Some of them told me to shut up and not say anything, but other friends supported me and complimented me. I did the right thing. So the moment I heard Chris's voice, my heart melted. I was exhausted from the sleepless nights, thinking repeatedly. I needed him badly. At that moment, I needed strong shoulders, a shoulder I could cry on, or strong big man hands to hug me and tell me while looking into my eyes that everything was going to be fine. With butterflies still in my stomach, the anticipation and eagerness to see my Chris was indescribable. I saw him, and my heart once again melted.

"You did the right thing," Chris said.

"I could not sleep at night. Knowing and not doing anything about it is not who I am."

"You are brave and so cute. Strong and sexy, baby."

The night was magical. We made love twelve times all night and morning. All twelve times were euphoric, passionate, and never-ending. I was so high that I could not feel the ground under my feet.

"I care about you deeply. You are the best woman I have ever met. I do not think I will ever meet someone like you. You are highly intellectual and beautiful inside out, woman. I respect you. I love you."

"I love you too. All these years, I cherished hopes that you and I will end up together."

"You are a special woman whom I am afraid I can't live up to, but I want you to give me another chance. And I will win your heart over!" said Chris.

I was getting stupid again and telling him, "I will give you a second chance because you deserve a second chance and because I have strong feelings for you for all seven years."

"I want to be with you, sweetie. I do not want to be with my wife. I have no feelings for her. She disrespects me. She does not love me. All she wants is my money," Chris said. "The past two years, I went through hell with her. She is bipolar. She punches me in my face in front of my kids. She is jealous every time her sister talks to me. She grabs the phone out of my hands and checks my phone. She is crazy."

He kept talking about his problems with his wife on and on. Afterward, he called me and told me he had got suspended from his clinic. The reason was he had been late a couple times. I felt bad and told him, "I should have kicked you out so you could make it on time. It is my fault for not kicking you out."

He came back for two days, and we stayed in bed for forty-eight hours. We made love for probably like twenty times. His big boy would not come down at all. He just kept going nonstop. I suggested him to be in the *Guinness World Records* book. Twenty-five times was a record in my experience.

"You see what you are doing to me, baby? Sex with you is amazing, and I can't get enough of you. Your vagina is like a pharmaceutical bottle. Your skin feels soft like silk." Chris sighed deeply and said in a very decisive tone of his voice, "That's it. I am getting divorced, baby, selling my apartment, setting up my own private practice, moving in with you, and I will live off my savings. I have $60,000 in my savings accounts. I will protect you and take care of you, my love. I will work two to three jobs if I am to provide you a good lifestyle. I will die for you. I will do anything for you. I love you so much." Chris held me all night long.

"I love you so much. I just do not trust you 100 percent—after you hurt me two years ago."

"I understand. I am sorry. I did terrible things to you. How much do you trust me?"

"Sixty-five percent. You have to prove your sincerity to me with your actions. Actions speak louder than words," I stated my trust issues with men.

"Sixty-five percent is good. I will work on the rest of 35 percent and prove to you how much I love you. Baby, imagine how our child would be: Korean, German, and Russian. Our child will be strong, highly intelligent, gorgeous, good, and well-brought-up. You will make a great mom. You make me the happiest man in the world."

"I love you more. We will be fundamentally happy and a powerful couple!"

A day later, Chris told me, "Obviously, my soon-to-be ex-wife felt something for the past two days and asked me to have dinner and talk with her."

Two hours later, Chris called and said she was not signing the divorce papers until they got marriage counseling. His family was super religious. It was so complicated. "I have to do everything to make their life best. I must protect my children."

He broke my heart again and played me again. He was just spending time with me until he figured out his situation. His thought process was like this: "If I get divorced, I will lose 50 percent of all my savings, 50 percent of my house. I have to pay my wife child support and alimony, and my super religious family will not talk to me ever again."

What happened was that the owner of the private clinic he got suspended from wanted him back, and his family gave him a lecture on the importance of family and being a good father. His wife was getting better and being super nice to him. I burst out crying and yelled, "I knew it. It was going to happen. But I wanted to take another chance with you!"

I felt huge pain and heartbreak caused by the same guy for the second time. I felt so stupid and hated myself then, so I texted him the following:

Chris, you are very cruel person. For the second time, you hurt me. You will get what you deserve. You will be miserable and unhappy for the rest of your life. Do not call me. Lose my number. No more of your bull-shit. You are an asshole, jerk, coward, stupid and a cheater. I am not getting involved with a married man. You are a cheater, liar and piece of shit. Because you needed me to please you, understand you and comfort you. I am a very prideful woman. I have done nothing but tried to understand you and developed deep feelings for you. You stepped all over my face and killed me. I despise you. Go away and sleep tight, underhanded coward and jerk. No wonder your wife beats you up. Now I get what you did to me and how you took advantage of me and played me. Here is what happened with you:

It has been a year and half since you and your wife are having problems. Your clinic job situation has been kind of shaky. That caused a lot of stress because you did not get enough sex. You know me as very nice, soft and classy woman. Well, this time I will turn into exactly the opposite. Later you will understand why.

You are an awful person. As soon as you got your clinic job back, your wife wants to work on your marriage, your dad is getting better and softer with you, you are good now, asshole. What about my heart? It aches so deep. Aren't you a super religious person? You are a sinner. Where and what is your religion now?

You go and fuck yourself.

Burn in Hell!

I was finally able to close this chapter for good. Looking at Chris now, seven years later, he is unhappily married, and he is in debt up to his ears ($100,000 in student loans).

Again, why do we women do this to ourselves? There are good guys out there. It is just hard to find them. There are great penises attached to greater guys.

Just to finally let it go, I wrote him a letter and emailed him. I am proud of my last email:

> Please do not call me anymore. You called me first two years later. Thank you for doing that. Thank you for all amazing nights. If you had not made love to me, told me all the wonderful things and one day later, went back to your family, I would not have known you. In all harsh reality, I do not know you. I have never known you either. Your actions and how you treated me have made me realize a lot of things about myself.
>
> I totally support your decision. Children are the most important thing in your life. Just try to find a joy in your life and be happy.
>
> You are not worthy of me at all.
>
> My conscious is clean. I am single. I have never cheated on my ex.
>
> Rest assured, I am not getting involved with a married man. I have never been and

never will. It is against my principles. And from now on you do not get to have any control over me.

Best of luck with everything and thank your wife on my behalf. I would shoot your ass if you cheated on me. I blocked your number and you do not exist for me. I am throwing you out of my life because it is the best way for you to save your marriage. Bye, bye, bye.

A seven-year unexplainable passionate chemistry between us was gone for good. He couldn't get to my level. I called his sperm Denied Access. I imagined Chris's sperm to be such jerks and full of shit that they couldn't be spotted and smelled by the strongest and smartest Cherry Blossom. She was blind, but she had a good teacher and smelled this kind of shit far away.

The thought process of Denied Access and how they act:

- Hyper, bouncy, and horny
- Loves her, but that is pretty much it
- "Since we are super religious, we can't get her pregnant. She is atheist. She will destroy our legacy."
- When he gets denied, he gets nervous, shakes, and gets closer to Cherry Blossom. Indecisive Denied Access panics, blows up, and dies.

Now I am not interested in dating. I have got big projects ahead of me. I have a 100 percent focus on making a difference and money to ensure my healthy and wealthy retirement.

Dating is getting to know someone. In the past, I jumped to bed quickly without knowing a person. Well, I was young and horny. I made a promise to myself: I will get to know him better, take it slow, and find out what reputation he has at work. Is he a good person to his parents and friends? What would he do if he were in my shoes? Do we have a lot in common? Can we enjoy the same things together?

I want to learn about contemporary and modern art and technological innovations, work on my two amazing projects, and most importantly, make a difference.

Life is not fair. I lost my dear friend Anastasia to brain cancer. It was heartbreaking and devastating for her parents and for all of us, her friends. She was the most beautiful person and the greatest friend; she was highly intelligent, always enthusiastic, young, pure, and genuine. I found out too late about her unhappy relationship with her boyfriend. Everyone who knew Anastasia should be aware of the truth about her boyfriend. Her boyfriend turned out to be the worst—a cruel and evil jerk and a possessive, obsessive maniac. If only people knew what he is and what he has done to her parents. I do not understand how earth can hold this evil jerk on the surface; he should have fallen six feet under the ground. I hope he gets punished for all the pain and cruelty he did to my friend and her parents.

I miss her a lot. All this time, I thought she was happy with her boyfriend. I wish we all talk about what we go through and not hold anything bad—any unhappiness, miseries, fears, and insecurities inside us. I encourage men and women to speak to your close friends, moms, sisters, brothers, or someone you feel open to talk about it. You will feel relieved, more confident, and get stronger to make the right decision.

In Anastasia's memory, there are two hundred tulips planted in Central Park by her coworkers, and her parents planted Christian Dior roses in their backyard. The Christian Dior roses resemble her heart and beauty. Rest in peace, sweet Anastasia.

I take every failure as a learning lesson and an opportunity to only move forward. And we all know that after hitting rock bottom, there is only one way, and it is going up—all the way up!

Take a journey to the pursuit of happiness with the good and right person with the right timing.

To be continued…

About the Author

ALEXANDRA KHAN WAS KOREAN RUSSIAN-BORN and raised in Uzbekistan by the most amazing and most loving parents. Her two great brothers, with their own families, reside in Siberia, Russia.

Right after graduating from the University of World Languages, Alexandra had a wonderful opportunity working for EU projects as an English-Russian interpreter. She had the most profound experience working and learning from brilliant individuals. Alexandra's early teenage dream was to become a journalist and diplomat. Her dream came true partially through working for EU projects and discovering the incredibly interesting European and Western world and mentality of diplomats, business consultants, and entrepreneurs. All that and working as an interpreter had enriched her knowledge and expanded horizons.

In 1999, she got discovered by Starwood Hotels in Tashkent. That was where and when she fell in love and found her passion in the hotel business and moved to the USA in 2001 in pursuit of her hotel career. Starwood Hotels supported Alexandra's transfer to the USA, for which she was very grateful.

She has not accomplished yet what she aims to. Very soon, you will hear about her. Alexandra worked in hotel operations, sales, and food and beverage and worked all her way up to director of sales and marketing for well-reputable hotel brands. Sixteen years later, the unstable job market and highly stressed work environment inspired her to write a book, get her business plan done, get another perspective of life, and learn to love herself more.

She is single. She enjoys fine dining, long walks on the beach, and classical music. She loves to dance and entertain guests.

"Enjoy the book! I am dedicating this book to my family, Anastasia, and all my readers. Thank you for reading my first book. I really hope you can relate to my stories—the stories that will make you laugh, love yourself more, and realize beautiful qualities about yourself. Be happy and live healthy!"